Lessons and Stories from The Journey

Reflections from The Life of A Joyful Priest

Fr. Mark S. Lawlor

Cover design by Joe Sade

ISBN: 9798446346691

Ordination as deacon,
October 8, 1994

Baptism in the jungle region of Peru,
Nueva Esperanza (New Hope),
2008

Dedication of Ministry Center and Chapel at
the Parish of St. Vincent de Paul, 2014

DEDICATION

This book is lovingly dedicated to three very important
women of my life:
My sister, Leslie Lynn Lawlor: 5/26/70 – 1/30/91
My mother, Josephine Anne Test Lawlor: 8/27/38 – 2/27/98
My grandmother, Mary Magdalene "Madge" Cecil Test:
1/05/1906 - 3/04/2002

Contents

Introduction

My first assignment as a priest was as the parochial vicar (assistant pastor) of Holy Family Church in Clemmons, North Carolina. It was an interesting clergy combination. I was just starting out, and my pastor, Fr. Walsh, was in his last year of parish ministry. He would be turning seventy the following summer and had already expressed his desire to retire. He was somewhat tired from declining health and displayed some residual stress from his many years of pastoral ministry. He was also planning to move to his late mother's former home in New York, and was often away making arrangements or simply doing things at the rectory. This situation meant that I was often the only priest in the office during the day. There was a lot of "on the job training" when calls came in, and I was brand new at this.

One afternoon, a call came into the office that was directed to me. The caller said, "I am not a Catholic but a Baptist. A friend of mine was raised Catholic in Brazil but for many years has expressed that she has no faith. She is now close to death from cancer. She just told me that she had a dream that she was riding a white horse to the church. Her dream led me to call you."

I was actually surprised by the call. The friend was taking the initiative to call the local Catholic parish. She had not been asked to make the call and request a priest to visit, and no one from the family had called the parish as is often the case with serious illnesses.

I was a little nervous about the situation when the woman gave me her friend's name, phone number, and address, and I made the call with some trepidation. An adult son answered. I related the phone conversation that I had had with his mother's friend and said that I would be willing to come to the home if that was what his mother desired. After a pause, her son responded, "Yes, you may come over."

This was in the days before GPS and the internet, so I found the address on a map and drove over, not knowing what to expect. I went to the door and an adult daughter answered. I explained why I had come, and she welcomed me in. I wasn't even sure if the mother knew that I was coming. She led me down the hall to the room where a very thin and frail woman was in a small hospital bed. I introduced myself and told her that her friend had called me. There was a period of silence, and then I asked, "Is it your desire to be reconciled with the Church?"

After another period of silence, she nodded her head indicating, with some reluctance, "Yes."

I began the Sacrament of the Anointing of the Sick, which was followed by the Prayer of Absolution and then, finally, Viaticum, the final Communion or food for the journey. As this was very early in my priestly ministry, I had not administered the Sacrament of Anointing that many times before. After the final blessing, she seemed very peaceful. As I prepared to leave, I told her daughter that I would be available if she wanted to call me back for any reason. I was thinking that perhaps the family might call the parish to schedule a funeral. After two days, I called the home. The daughter answered, and I asked, "How is your mother doing?"

She said, "She died shortly after you left."

At that moment, I became much more profoundly aware of the role of a priest. Ultimately, a priest is trying to help people to make the transition from this life to eternal life. Of course, priests have assistance. I was at that home because her Baptist friend had called me and because her children accepted a priest's offer for a pastoral visit.

For many years, I was home in Salisbury on my day off and would concelebrate the morning Mass in my home parish with my mentor, Fr. Thomas Clements. When I was ordained, he was celebrating his fortieth anniversary. I told him that story the next week, and he remarked, "Mark, that will keep you going in the priesthood for the next twenty years!"

Well, I just celebrated twenty-five years.

My intention for this book is to share stories such as this one and to reflect on the wonder of Divine Providence and my call to serve in this vocation. As a seminarian, I came across the book *The Lord and I: Vignettes from the Life of a Parish Priest* by Msgr. Vincent Fecher in our school library. I enjoyed the book very much, and I thought that most priests probably have similar stories. Perhaps, some of them are related in homilies or retreats, but I suspect that many of them will never be written down. I wrote to Msgr. Fecher and thanked him for his book. He wrote back, and, in his letter, he conveyed that he had written the book for people like me. That small book encouraged me to begin this book project as a seminarian. After about twenty-eight years, and having now passed my sixtieth birthday, I have finally decided to try to bring this endeavor to some conclusion. My purpose is primarily to reflect on my journey to the priesthood and on my life as a priest. The stories you will read are all true. In certain cases, I have changed names and condensed dialogues, but the heart of each story is presented as I remember it. This work is not intended to be a textbook, but I include some things that I have learned over the years, which I desire to share with the readers. (A priest is also called to be a teacher.)

The road so far has been fascinating, and there have been many instances where I have certainly known and seen the Lord's peace and grace. I have come to trust that the Lord is never very far away. Many faces have greeted me along the way, and each holds a special place in my heart. Many people to whom I intended to minister have actually ministered to me. Some of them have already been called to their eternal reward, and I hope that their souls are in peace.

I know that I have been greatly blessed on this journey. It is my hope that by sharing my stories and reflections, others may also reflect on their own journey of faith. In the end we have nothing to fear if we believe what St. Paul wrote to the Christian community of Rome:

"If God is for us, who can be against us?" (Romans 8:31).

I truly believe that God is for us.

Mark Stephen Lawlor
August 4, 2021,
Memorial of St. John Vianney

First Holy Communion in 1969

CHAPTER 1

A Life of Contrasts

So to them, he addressed this parable. "What man among you having a hundred sheep and losing one of them would not leave the ninety-nine in the desert and go after the lost one until he finds it?"
—LUKE 15:3–4

I n my early twenties, I had the appearance of having a pretty good life. I had been blessed with good health; I had a seemingly secure and well-paying job with the Department of the Navy; I had a nice apartment; I was living in the beautiful city of Charleston, South Carolina; and I was spending a lot of time with a lovely, caring, and athletic woman. At times, relatives and friends expressed their admiration of my seemingly charmed life, and a friend commented that I *had it all.* Their perception was, however, highly inaccurate. In retrospect, I know that I did not have it all. I was severely lacking in what truly matters, and I was yearning for something deeper but was unsure of where to turn.

My life was one of contrasts. I possessed many material possessions, but these did nothing to nurture a spiritual life. I had memberships in professional societies and in social and health clubs, but I was only on the periphery of God's community of faith—the Church. In fact, I was just a step away from being outside of the Church altogether. I had many friends and acquaintances, but lacked a close relationship with Jesus Christ, our Lord, Savior, and Brother. I had been presented with a number of educational opportunities, in part due to my middle-class and stable upbringing. I had graduated from college with a Bachelor of Science in Mechanical Engineering, and I had a number of interests in the realm of science and technology. I tried to remain up to date in the field of engineering and related fields by reading at least five monthly periodicals, and I attempted to keep up with current events by reading a daily newspaper. I was certainly not a scholarly or brilliant person, but, perhaps, I was considered well-educated and informed in some areas.

Yet, despite my education and study, I was, in reality, an ignorant and unenlightened person. I had truly missed the things of higher value. For instance, I spent no time reading and reflecting on God's Holy Word in Sacred Scripture, and I had practically no knowledge of salvation history, Sacred Tradition, the sacraments, and the Church's social and moral teachings. These are the foundation stones on which one builds an authentic Christian life. There is a difference between knowledge and faith and between wisdom and learning. God was preparing to show me His truth, and He was inviting me to come into His light.

Another contrast of my life was that while I was physically strong and healthy, I was very weak with regards to living a morally sound life and overcoming temptation. I was also weak in standing steadfast in the Faith and speaking out against evil, and there were many times that I tried to avoid or ignore my conscience. I endeavored to portray an appearance of independence, confidence, and competence while there existed within me a hunger and yearning for a true spiritual life and dependence on God. As I reflect upon these contrasts, I am able to identify with the second verse of Psalm 63:

> *Oh God, you are my God—it is you I seek!*
> *For you my body yearns: for you my soul thirsts,*
> *In a land parched, lifeless, and without water.*

I was dry and weary and unsure of where I was going.

CHAPTER 2

Where Do We Go From Here?

*. . . and that they may return to their senses out of
the devil's snare, where they are entrapped by him,
for his will.*
—2 TIMOTHY 2:26

T he Good Shepherd had not, however, forgotten about one of His lost sheep. I now know that when one is close to the bottom, there is the potential for a conversion experience and new growth. Consider the Parable of the Prodigal Son in Luke 15. The lost son experienced his conversion while he was feeding the unclean swine and realized that they were eating better than he was. He thought of the family and home that he had been all too eager to leave behind. Scripture has it that he *came to his senses.*

At the age of twenty-three, when so much seemed to be going well, I was spiritually drying out. I had pretty much fallen away from the Church at this point in my life, and I even harbored a bit of contempt for most organized and institutional religions, which I saw as being opulent and hypocritical. Although I never doubted the existence of a loving and merciful God, I felt that these institutions had somehow strayed from God's message.

My material possessions and my social and romantic relationships could not fill the void in me that longed to know God. The contrasts in my life and my confusion at this time set the stage for a major turning point from which there would be no turning back.

About this time, James, a very close friend of mine since junior high school, called me from North Carolina. James had been a professional athlete and had always lived life to the fullest. He excitedly explained a recent dream that he had had in which he saw Jesus leading him and the Apostles along the edge of a cliff, and then the Lord turned to him and asked, "Are you ready to follow me as a minister?"

I clearly recall my friend's enthusiasm on that phone call as he proclaimed with a sincere conviction, "It's all true! The Bible is all true!" It was evident that my friend honestly believed that he had received a divine message, but I was perhaps a little skeptical since he had come up with some other enthusiastic stories in the past.

A few weeks passed, and then, on a weekend trip to my hometown, James, another close friend named Claude, and I met at a bar for a few beers. Our discussion that night quickly turned to religion, and it was lively exchange. James was still on his spiritual high from his dream, and he had been attending a small Presbyterian church. He had also been spending a great deal of time reading Scripture and memorizing chapters and verses. He challenged Claude and me to leave the Catholic Church and to go somewhere such as a rural Presbyterian church where we would get "the Word." Now Claude and I had been classmates in our parochial elementary school and had been altar servers years earlier in our youth, but we didn't really know our Faith. That night, our ignorance of the Church was evident, and we were quite inadequate to counter the enthusiastic claims of James, which, in fact, were beginning to sound rather convincing.

From my work with the federal government, I had concluded that the bigger an institution is, the less efficient it becomes due to the corresponding bureaucracy. I wondered where that left the Catholic Church, which is perhaps the largest organization in history. I openly wondered if the Church was in touch with the intent of her founder, Jesus Christ. My conclusions were not very complimentary.

Upon returning to Charleston, I reflected on James's words to find a church where "the Word" was preached. I thought of shopping around but did not really know where to begin. The irony is that while I never did search for a Bible-based congregation in the country, I would actually confirm James as a Catholic about fifteen years later.

There was nostalgia in my heart for Catholicism. I thought of my six years in parochial schools, my First Communion, my Confirmation, and the years as an altar server. Those days seemed so long ago. I also thought of the living example of faith of my grandmother, Mary Magdalene Test.

I decided that I would attend one more Mass before I began searching for another Christian community. In my immature mind, I was going to give the Catholic Church *one more chance*. I intended to try to pay attention to see if I would "get anything out of the Mass." Since the pastor of the local parish was not a very dynamic preacher, I did not have high hopes that anything significant was going to happen.

I have since learned not to be surprised by unexpected moments of grace.

A young server (with the glasses and hair) in 1974

But a future priest?
(Not likely)

CHAPTER 3

The Mission with Fr. Earl Larson: A Herald of the Word

It is the hour now for you to awake from sleep.
For our salvation is nearer now than when we first
believed.
—ROMANS 13:11

I began to "see the light" after a Sunday evening Mass in the first week of March, 1985. I had not set foot in a church since Christmas, and I was unsure of my place and future. It was my intention to attend Mass and to be open to inspiration. At the time, I did not even realize that the Church was in the liturgical season of Lent. I had missed Ash Wednesday that year.

I was often late for Mass when I did go, but, fortunately, I was on time that evening. That was the first miracle since I had spent much of the day at the beach! Before Mass began, a priest wearing a white robe charged down the center aisle, went to the ambo, and addressed the congregation. He stated that if we wanted to learn about such topics as the history of the Church, the Ten Commandments, the creation of the cosmos, and evolution, then we should attend the mission this week that would begin immediately after Mass. I thought to myself, *This sounds pretty interesting. Maybe I should give this Faith one more hour after Mass.* I remembered that I had already made plans to spend the evening with my girlfriend, but, by the end of Mass, I had decided to stay for the first talk of the mission.

The priest was Fr. Earl Larson from an abbey in the Midwest, and, after Mass, he wasted no time getting right into his message. The first night, he covered the creation accounts of Genesis, the Big Bang Theory of science, the Fall of humanity, the call of Abraham, the coming of the Savior, the first apostles, the birth of the Church, and the vision of the Emperor Constantine prior to the Battle of the Milvian Bridge in the year 312 AD. I thought, *Wow! That was an exciting tour through salvation and Church history.* I decided to go back the next night and then the next three after that. My girlfriend even joined me on a couple of those evenings. I don't think that I had ever participated in religious services on five consecutive nights ever before in my life. On the fifth night, the mission closed with Benediction of the Blessed Sacrament and the Sacrament of Reconciliation. I truly felt the presence of Christ as I prayed in front of His Body and as I received the gift of His peace and mercy through Absolution. I had been long overdue for a good confession.

That mission marked a turning point in my life. It changed my whole outlook. At the end of the week, I felt as though the blinders had been removed my eyes. I was energized by the Holy Spirit and suddenly able to see much clearer. With regard to the Church, I no longer saw a cold and materialistic institution but the Family of God. And as all families have tensions and quarrels, so does the Church. The timing was amazing, and, upon further reflection, I believe that I was led to attend that Mass prior to that mission, which I knew nothing about. Perhaps, if I had gone to a morning Mass that Sunday, I would not have returned for the evening session.

Shortly thereafter, I officially joined the parish and, from that moment on, I made it a priority to attend Sunday Mass each week. I also began to contribute via the envelopes that I had received shortly after joining the parish in lieu of the "spare change method." It was somewhat ironic when I finally realized that the Church is the living Family of God and the Body of Christ. I can remember that, prior to the mission, I was doing a lot of long-distance cycling on weekends. On one such Sunday morning, I took off on the coastal highway for a fifty miler. Along the way, on that beautiful morning, I passed many small churches and saw their members parking their cars and entering for their services. I remember looking at some of them in a condescending way and thinking: *These poor folks are going to church. They really should just get a bicycle and go riding. That would certainly boost their spirituality.*

The transition from my former state to that of an active follower of Christ was not without its challenges. Try slamming on the brakes of your car and changing direction. You will certainly feel a major lurch. My previous priorities and lifestyle had become obsolete and were in need of a major overhaul.

One obvious contradiction with my rediscovered faith was my relationship with a recently separated woman who was going through a contentious divorce. There was a strong bond of love between us, and I really did not know what to do with the situation. I read the little question and answer catechism that I had bought at the mission, and I knew that I had to reform my life. Attempting to develop some self-discipline, I tried to control my emotions around her. This period was one of the most gut-wrenching times of my whole life. She could not grasp my internal struggle or the meaning or reason for the sudden coolness of my demeanor, and it hurt her greatly. We continued to see each other, and we had some good times, but an emotional strain developed between us, almost like a sense of tragedy. I felt as though I was going through a major earthquake. Although our love was strong, and we were very compatible in many ways, marriage was never something that I seriously considered. In addition to her need for an annulment, there were other complicating factors including the difference in our ages and the stressful situation that she had with her own children.

With the help of God's grace, I was coming to grips with my faith and the corresponding moral decisions. It was what the Lord was calling me to do. It was a hard thing to talk about, and I kept a lot to myself. My rediscovered faith was not something that I felt comfortable discussing with my laid-back friends, who enjoyed going to the beach and to parties, or even with my immediate family. They had not changed, and I did not think that they would understand my new outlook on life.

I remember being invited to the bachelor party of a co-worker during this time period and I actually lied when I said that I couldn't make it because my car was in the shop.

As a type of spiritual coincidence (or rather Providence), my grandmother sent me a copy of *The New Jerusalem Bible* for my twenty-fourth birthday, and it arrived just a couple of weeks after the mission. My grandmother had sent me religious gifts in the past, but this one could not have arrived at a better time. When I received the Bible, I was totally ignorant of its contents, but, as I inspected it, I was impressed by the text and the footnotes. I immediately began with the Gospel of Matthew, and I read for about fifteen minutes each night, usually in bed. After about three months, I had read the entire New Testament. I had never realized there was so much there! These words truly became "Words of life" for me, and I saw the timelessness of the inspired Word of God and its application for my troubled life. Some passages literally hit me "between the eyes" (as one of my former parishioners used to say). Other than a few parts of the books, such as Genesis and Exodus, I had never sat down and read much from the Bible. In fact, I was quite lost when it came to the Scriptures. I recall that, after seeing the movie *King David* a year or so earlier, I had unsuccessfully searched for the passage that told the story of the battle between David and Goliath. I also remember wondering once, after the epistle reading at Mass, *Who is St. Paul and why is he writing all these letters?* With my new Bible with its extensive footnotes and book introductions, I began to learn about and to love the Sacred Scriptures. This connection with the Word of God has never faded over these thirty-six years.

I was attending Mass at my local parish, getting acquainted with God's revealed Word, reading my simple catechism, and trying to put my moral life in order. Surely God was pleased that I was back on the road that leads to salvation. The lost sheep had been led back to the flock. I wrote to Fr. Larson and thanked him for sharing so much during the mission, and I assured him that it had been very beneficial for my spiritual life.

What could possibly happen next?

CHAPTER 4

The Call of the Lord

Jesus said to them, "Come after me, and I will make you fishers of men."
—MARK 1:17

It was now two years since my graduation from college. I had a comfortable salary and was preparing to buy a house in a new subdivision on James Island in the city of Charleston. I looked forward to having my own place after having rented apartments for two years. I was also pleased to learn that I would receive a tax break by itemizing my mortgage interest.

Buying a new home was exciting. I had heard of this new subdivision from a coworker. I went over by myself and toured the model homes. There was a corner lot available, and it seemed like a great idea. I impulsively signed a contract to buy the lot and future home. I then picked out my floorplan, colors, light fixtures, carpet, and linoleum. They made it as smooth as buying a car. Working for the government made getting the loan very easy. My girlfriend couldn't believe it. After I told her about signing the contract, she exclaimed, "You did all that? And even picked out your colors?" Shortly thereafter, construction on my new home began. I often worked second shift so that I could observe some of the construction during the day. Within three months, the home was ready, and I moved in. At the closing, I felt as though I had really accomplished something. At the young age of twenty-four, I had a home, even though it was far from mine as I had just agreed to pay $538. per month for the next thirty years! Wasn't home ownership part of the American dream? Then, out of nowhere, it happened.

A voice that I initially thought was a simple case of comic relief from an over-stressed mind spoke to me. The voice said, *Now that you're back on track, would you consider taking another step?* Was this a call to ministry like James had received? And, if it was, why me, and why now? I was quite happy in my new little home. I thought that if the Lord was really calling me, it surely was bad timing. He could have called me before I bought the home, which would have saved me a lot of trouble.

What did this message mean? At that time, I had no idea and could not even imagine where the road would lead.

CHAPTER 5

The Initial Discernment

To you, O Lord, I lift up my soul, my God, in you I
trust.
—PSALM 25:1

U nlike some of my contemporaries in the seminary, I had never thought about a religious vocation at any time in my life. I had some mechanical aptitude for working with tools, and so the pursuit of a degree in mechanical engineering in college made sense. On the day I graduated from college, I remember hearing a classmate say, "I look forward to getting into management."

That sounded so strange to me after all of the technical courses that we had taken. I remember thinking, *I would much rather work with machines than with people!*

A religious vocation was just another area about which I knew very little. After hearing this invitation from God, I again wrote to Fr. Larson and requested his guidance and counsel. He responded with words of wisdom, and he encouraged me to pray about it. He also gave my name to the vocation director of his abbey who sent me some vocation literature. About the same time, I received a catalog in the mail with descriptions of various religious orders. To this day, I am unsure how I came to receive this booklet. Over the course of several weeks, I filled out and sent in about six or seven cards from the booklet requesting more information on some of the religious communities. Soon thereafter, I began to receive mail by the bushel! I now know that most vocation directors take seriously the requests for more information. I started to receive calls at night from vocation personnel asking if I was receiving their newsletters, if I had any questions, or if I was still interested. On one such occasion, a Marist priest called and asked if I was interested in participating in a vocation retreat in New Orleans. Initially, I was thinking of how to politely decline, until he mentioned that he would pay my airfare and pick me up at the airport. *Why not?* I thought. I certainly had never been to New Orleans, although I had heard about it. I decided to go. The retreat was to be held at a former noviate house for a religious order of sisters on the bayou. Before the retreat, we were able to do a little sightseeing in the city. I recall seeing the famous Bourbon Street and having my photo taken in front of the street sign.

On the retreat, there were several vocation directors from religious orders of men and woman and also a diocesan priest. There were probably about twenty to twenty-five participants at the retreat. This was one of my first encounters with others who were also considering a religious vocation. At the time, I was thinking that perhaps I could be a foreign missionary or a teacher. I remember asking the diocesan priest what he was doing. He said that he had been a priest for five years, that he was in a parish, and that he really enjoyed parish work. I remember thinking to myself, *Poor soul. He likes parish work?* It seems funny to me now as that is all that I have done for the past twenty-six years as a priest! I was also invited to a vocation retreat at an abbey in Wisconsin. I had an idea that I could study under Fr. Larson and carry on his work of preaching missions and teaching the Faith throughout the world. I had good experiences on these religious excursions but there was a tug of war going on within me. The transition to a life of grace is not always smooth and some virtues seemed at times to be just a distant goal. I've since learned that conversion is a lifetime process.

While I was unsure of my future. I was quite sure that I would not remain at my position with the naval shipyard for a career, although I enjoyed the field of engineering. I thought that an ideal compromise would be a religious vocation as a brother while continuing the practical tasks of engineering. I thought that it would be great to do something like design and build churches or parochial schools as a member of a religious community, or maybe just work in the boiler room or shop of a monastery and fix things. I explored the possibilities of becoming a brother, but the communities I contacted did not offer quite what I was looking for. I initially had doubts about the priesthood because I considered myself unworthy. Priests do holy things, and I did not consider myself a holy person. Again, I wrote to Fr. Larson requesting his guidance, and he assured me that no one is worthy of Holy Orders, but that it certainly is a calling.

After much prayer and reflection, I gradually saw that I was being called to the Sacrament of Holy Orders. I often attended the early morning Mass in my parish and would then spend a few minutes in the Blessed Sacrament chapel asking for direction. I found myself praying, *Yes Lord, I will be a priest, but where? You must show me where to go.*

The Jesuits were very attractive to me based on their commitment to education and their history as missionaries. I was also interested in other societies, religious orders, and the Diocese of Charleston, South Carolina, which had become my home for the past several years. I had become friends with Fr. Larry McInerny, who was the parochial vicar of my parish, Blessed Sacrament. He was also the vocation director for the diocese. I remember him telling me once, "Parish ministry is the front-line of the Church."

I have come to believe that that statement is true.

CHAPTER 6

The Decision and Move

*Jesus turned and saw them following him and said
to them, "What are you looking for?" They said to
him, "Rabbi (which translated means Teacher),
where are you staying?" He said to them, "Come and
you will see."*
—JOHN 1:38–39

Sometimes, I would lay on my sofa in the evening and look up through the skylight. I would ask myself, *Am I able to just walk out the door and leave all of this behind?* It was an internal struggle. I didn't want to be in my sixties wondering if I should have tried. Just as I was beginning to wonder if I would ever receive a clear sign, I received a mailing from The Glenmary Home Missioners, which described their candidacy program. It looked great! The program enabled one to get hands-on ministry experience in a small parish or mission, to work in community based social services such as literacy or wood-cutting, to study pre-theology and Sacred Scripture, and to travel to regions in the South and Southwest to experience different cultures with their corresponding challenges and concerns.

I thought that the program was truly the answer to my prayers. I had had very little experience in any of these areas, and I projected that after the nine-month program I would know better the direction of my future. I was also confident that I could always get a job and survive if it didn't work out. I think that I called Glenmary the day that I received the mailing and spoke with Brother Jack, the vocation director. I told him to go ahead and sign me up. Brother Jack seemed a little surprised. Although I had been receiving mailings from Glenmary for about a year, this was my first response. He explained that it would be better if I was able to spend a little time with them so that we could get to know each other a better before any commitment was made. He suggested that I try to make it to the upcoming volunteer week and/or the following discernment week. I guess that made sense to me, although I still thought that their program was the answer to my prayers. When I called, however, I didn't really understand that Glenmary was not just providing a "missionary boot camp" for poor souls like me who weren't sure where to pursue their vocation.

I read the candidacy brochure over and over, and then I began to go back through the back issues of their magazine, *The Glenmary Challenge*. I was thoroughly convinced that I was going to be a Glenmarian. I had about two months before the volunteer week, so I had to get busy. Quitting work would not be a problem as I had been threatening to leave for a couple of years. I did have to sell my little cookie-cutter house, and that was something that gave me some anxiety. I figured that I could always just move out and default on the loan. The bank could then just foreclose the house and sell it. I figured that I wouldn't be needing a house as I headed for the home missions, and, at that time, I wasn't too concerned about my credit score. I mentioned my leaving to a coworker and good friend, and he said that he was interested in buying my home as a rental. We agreed on an equity price and had the loan transferred, which was actually very easy. Things were falling in place.

It was time to resign my position at the shipyard. I was leaving the world of two-hundred-million-dollar nuclear submarine overhauls to embrace the simple life in small towns that weren't even on some maps. Looking back at my five years at "The Yard," I know that I had been compensated well for my work, and that I was fortunate to have been employed during a national recession. I know that there is no such thing as a perfect job, but the shipyard was not fulfilling for me most of the time. When it came time for my official check-out, I had to fill out a government form that listed my history of work and forwarding address, and it had places for the different departments to check off that I had turned in my hard hat and other equipment. [I still have my steel toe work shoes from that period.] The form had a box that requested the reason for departure. Someone, for example, may write something like retirement or other employment opportunity in the box. I simply wrote, "Current position is not my calling." I remember that as I made it to the last stop where I turned in my parking permit and badge, the attendant saw the reason, smiled, and said, "You don't like it here, do you?" I nodded my head in agreement, and he remarked that he appreciated honesty. Little did I know then how much more fulfilling my life would soon be. As I walked to my car, I experienced a tremendous sense of freedom, and I really had a skip in my step as I embarked on my new mission. I cashed in my Civil Service retirement account, which greatly helped me as I would have little to no income for the next seven years.

The volunteer week was based in a small town in Eastern Kentucky in a socially poor area. Glenmary had a bought some rural property there known as "The Farm" and had set up a couple of barns for volunteers with bunk beds. There were about twenty-five volunteers, many of whom were college students from the Northeast. We spent the week visiting a nursing home, helping to build a home for a poor family, visiting some country folks, going to a rural holiness revival, attending Mass in a small local parish, and praying and singing around the campfire at night. About six or seven of us stayed on for the following discernment week, and we went to Glenmary's headquarters in Cincinnati to go through the formal application process. I survived the physical and psychological testing and the interviews. I just knew that I would be accepted, since I was convinced that God had invited me and set it up. I had just resigned from my position at the shipyard, sold my house, and given away or sold numerous possessions. I did not have a "Plan B." I was accepted and, after a summer with travels to Europe and Canada, I prepared for a journey to Hartford, Kentucky to begin the candidacy program.

I had intended to leave from my parent's house in the afternoon and arrive in Hartford some 540 miles away around midnight. I was kind of on a night driving kick, and I enjoyed the cooler temperatures and the reduced traffic. As soon as I filled my old car up with gas, I noticed a gas leak. I sincerely could not believe it, and, when I got under the car, I saw that the gas hose was cracked above the tank. It was one that would be hard to get to, remove, and replace, and I dreaded changing it. I rushed on my bicycle to buy a replacement hose at a local auto parts store. As I worked to make the replacement, a summer-long drought came to end with a tremendous thunderstorm while I was underneath my car with all of my tools spread out on my parent's driveway. I shouted, "Why?" This trip had not yet begun, and I was already getting off on the wrong track! My father offered to help me, but, at that moment, I was just too stressed to accept his kind offer.

I was soaking wet, dirty, and smelling of gas, but, after getting cleaned up and fully packed, I finally headed out at about 9:00 pm for the journey. I probably should have waited until the next morning, but I was so keyed up that I doubt I would have slept very well that night. I did fine until about 4:00 am, and then I was almost falling asleep at the wheel. I pulled off the Interstate and slept in my car in an apartment complex parking lot for a short time. I was totally drained when I arrived at the Hartford candidacy house at about 7:15 am. As I pulled into the driveway, my stressed-out and severely fatigued psyche give me a hard dose of reality by taunting me: *You quit your job, you sold or gave away your possessions, you have no home, and now you're at a religious house of formation in Kentucky! Do you know what you have done??!!*

I knew that I was in need of sleep, and, after a short nap, I was comfortable in my new home, the Hartford House. Since that day, I have never regretted that midnight drive and move, or had another moment when I seriously questioned or doubted my journey to the priesthood.

I remain convinced that I have answered a call from the Lord.

CHAPTER 7

Candidacy

God chose the foolish of the world to shame the wise,
and God chose the weak of the world to shame the
strong,
—1 CORINTHIANS 1:27

WELCOME TO HARTFORD, HOME OF 2000 HAPPY PEOPLE AND A FEW SOREHEADS
—Highway sign welcoming travelers
to Hartford, Kentucky

L arge signs boast of an overwhelming happiness as they welcome travelers and visitors to Hartford, Kentucky. In this small town in Western Kentucky, the Glenmary Home Missioners had their candidacy house of formation. The large ten-bedroom house at 300 Peach Alley had a colorful history as reported in the local oral tradition. For example, it had once served as a boarding house, and some of the neighbors reported that it was one of those places where a traveler could get a drink and maybe even gamble a bit, even though it was a dry county. I heard that a person had been shot in the front lawn during those days of revelry. Once, while browsing in a local pawn shop, the worker asked me where I lived, as it was very small town. When I told him, he took off his cap and showed me a scar on his forehead that he said he had received at the Hartford House.

Glenmary had bought the house in very poor condition and several of the Glenmary brothers had renovated it in a grand way. The old wash house had been converted into a lovely chapel where I used to love to pray. The altar had been made from two large tree stumps. There was even a real sense of gratitude among the neighbors for what Glenmary had done to the house. Apparently, the idea of having a Catholic house of studies in the neighborhood wasn't quite as bad as having a house of gambling, drinking, and who knows what else. The ecumenical movement has come a long way. Perhaps, in an earlier day, some might have preferred the wild bunch to Catholics!

A Glenmary priest also served as the pastor of the parish in the neighboring town of Beaver Dam and ministered to the two small Catholic missions in the area. It was truly mission territory with all the typical characteristics such as a small percentage of Catholics (1% or so), a high percentage of unchurched people, and a relatively high unemployment rate with many folks suffering from despair and low self-esteem, which, of course, fuel other problems. Apparently, at one time, strip mining for coal had been a major trade in that area, and many men had quit high school to work in the mines. With the closing of the mines, a number of these men were out of work without a high school diploma or marketable job skills, and some had health problems as well. The surviving jobs in the area were highly sought after with literally hundreds of people applying for a few positions. One native man told me that the area had once been quite prosperous due to oil wells. He even mentioned that, largely due to oil revenues, they didn't experience "that little thing called the Great Depression." Hartford was quite a different place for me, and it would be my home for nine months.

I had just experienced five really good years in Charleston, South Carolina, a coastal city with lots of charm. I had enjoyed the beauty of the rivers and the ocean, running on the beach, cycling the scenic roads past old plantation houses and marshes, walking the historic downtown, dining outdoors with great scenery, seeing lots of boats, attending Mass in the beautiful cathedral, and spending lots of time with coworkers and friends. While the positives far outweighed the negatives, Charleston was, however, a mixed bag for me. Hartford did not, for example, have the rush-hour traffic, crowds at most places, e.g., the DMV or a bank, parking nightmares, dynamic thunder-storms and hurricanes, gnats, and drawbridge delays. I guess that every place has a downside that tourists or short-term visitors may not see or simply overlook. For all of the charm and history of Charleston, it really didn't take me long to get adjusted to life in a small town in rural Kentucky. At that time, the Charleston Naval Base and Shipyard had more employees and dependents than did the five hundred square miles of Ohio County of which Hartford is the county seat. The pace of life was definitely slower, but it was a quiet place and a welcomed change of pace!

In the candidacy house, there were five other candidates and two directors, Fr. Mike and Brother Dennis ("Bro. D"). While living in a different state and in a different cultural perspective did not pose any significant problems for me, living in a religious community did have its challenges. I had suddenly gone from five years of living alone to community life. I had really enjoyed my independence and the freedom of coming and going as I pleased—outside of work requirements. Then, suddenly, I was being given "chores" to do and a schedule of when I was expected to be at house meetings, when I was assigned to cook, to wash dishes, and to clean house. Perhaps, because of my mechanical background, I was also designated as the "car bubba." Over the years, I had gained a lot of experience working on my own clunkers, but now, in addition to my own car, I was tasked with the maintenance of the five house cars. It seemed as though every time I turned around, one of the house cars was due for an oil change or a minor repair, and Bro. D was a stickler for precise routine maintenance. Sometimes, I felt as though I was running a small auto garage.

When I lived alone, I usually just cooked and cleaned when it was convenient for me. Sometimes, I would just pick up some dinner on the way home from my workout at the health club. I'll admit that a schedule connected with community living initially caused me some resentment. For example, there were some beautiful days when I would have preferred to have gone cycling in the afternoon and then just fixed a sandwich for a late supper in lieu of having to spend a couple of hours in the kitchen working from Bro. D's menu, usually consisting of meat, mashed potatoes, and pie, which was to be followed verbatim. I would later spend five years around the monks of St. Meinrad and gain a greater appreciation for community living, but I've always remained somewhat of a free spirit when it comes to house schedules. Nevertheless, I grew a lot spiritually and personally amid the challenges, chores, and responsibilities of the Hartford House. Before then, I don't think that I had ever peeled a potato or baked a pie!

The real fulfillment came from the ministerial and outreach opportunities. We spent two days a week taking classes in Scripture and spirituality at Brescia College in Owensboro, which is run by the Ursuline sisters. On the other days, we were expected to be involved with some community outreach and parish programs. With six candidates in the house, we quickly became fairly well known in the community. My brother candidates formed a band and called themselves "The Flying Tators." They played for the area nursing homes and for parish youth programs and the like. They were really very good, and I was proud of them. They put a lot of joyful energy into their music. A few of us visited a juvenile reform school and spent some time with the troubled teens there. We also taught in literacy programs and helped the poor and elderly with yard work, moving furniture, minor house repairs, and cutting wood. Visiting shut-ins was also an important element of our presence. I remember visiting a nursing home once where I chatted with a woman who was 107 years old and who was a great-great-great grandmother! I had hardly done any volunteer work in my life, and these were great experiences. I was amazed at how many needs and opportunities there were even in this sparsely populated area.

I worked one day a week at a sheltered workshop. My only sister had been born with Down Syndrome, and I had always been impressed with those who had worked with her in Special Education and those who volunteered in the Special Olympics. Working at this workshop was something that I had really wanted to do, and I had many good experiences with these special people of God. I also taught in the Faith Formation program at the Catholic mission in Morgantown. I usually only had a couple of children in my class, but this was probably good since it was my first experience teaching the Faith. I became good friends with Franciscan Sister Marcan Freking, the pastoral administrator of the mission. I learned a lot from her quiet and non-threatening approach to ministry. While there were very few Catholics in the area, and only about fifteen families in the Catholic mission, she had the respect of everyone that I met during my time there.

Fr. Mike once said that the candidacy program was like a survey course. That was a true assessment. We visited people and missions in Appalachia, Mississippi, Arkansas, and Texas. In Trammel, VA, we visited a community of about seventy-five humble homes that was just receiving internal plumbing. I was surprised at the time that these conditions still existed in the United States. In Texas, we visited a Hispanic family and I actually made my first tortilla!

While I have a collage of memories from that year, some people, events, and places stand out in a way that I know I will never forget.

The late John Claise was one of the more memorable folks. He came by the candidacy house several times a week for a cup of coffee and conversation. John lived alone on a farm close by and had been in declining health following a couple of strokes. He was a trustworthy man, and he was interested in our studies and activities. He usually began a conversation by saying, "Howdy, neighbors," and he would respond affirmatively to a question by saying, "*Oui*, that means yes." John's heritage was from the French speaking section of Belgium. He was a gentle man and very likable. In short, he was very *neighborly*. Years later, I would meet a couple of John's relatives who lived in the St. Meinrad area near where John was born. The first time that I met John, he mentioned that one of the candidates from the previous class used to come over to bush hog his land. I just nodded my head, since at the time, I had no idea what bush hogging meant.

Another great one was the late Shirley Hines, who is perhaps the most unique person I have ever met. When I think of her, the memories bring a smile to my face. Shirley was an African American widow in her seventies. She was Pentecostal and lived alone in a little clapboard shack that was heated by an old cast iron wood stove. Several stray cats lived behind her house hoping to receive some scraps. She practically knew the entire Bible by heart, which came from many years of dedicated daily reading and prayer. She said that she did no work before 10:00 am, "Because that's the Lord's time, child!"

Since our class was the third candidacy group in Hartford, we often continued where previous classes had been before. Somehow, Fr. Mike had met Shirley, and she took a real liking to him and often phoned "Brother Mike"—in strict obedience to "call no one on earth your father" (Mt. 23:9)—whenever she needed to go to the store, or needed some firewood, or needed help for any other reason. Well, Shirley called the house soon after our candidacy year began and explained that the city had sent her a letter explaining that, if she did not have her yard mowed and cleaned up, the city would send a crew over and then send her a bill for the work. She was concerned because she was very poor and would be unable to pay the bill if the city did this job.

We arranged to go over to her house the following Saturday morning, and we arrived with a couple of push mowers, a sickle, some clippers, and a couple of weed eaters. Fr. Mike introduced us to Shirley. She then stated that we must pray before we start. She quoted extensively from Scripture and then prayed for our safety. She then went into a discourse about her letter from the city. I remember her saying that "they are just trying to get people's land out from under 'em."

The lawn appeared as though it had been neglected for a year or more. The grass and weeds were several feet high in some areas and the mowers just couldn't cut it. After several hard hours of work, the front lawn finally looked presentable. We decided that this ought to satisfy the city for the time being and that the backyard could wait for another day.

When Shirley saw that we were packing up, she came out and excitedly exclaimed, "You're not leaving, are you?" We replied that the front yard now looked pretty good and that the back could wait for another time. She resisted our reasoning and said, "We must obey civil authority." She then paraphrased Romans 13:1 by saying, "God has established the earthly rulers, and we are subject to them."

Fr. Mike knew Shirley pretty well and decided to challenge her passage from Scripture with another by saying, "It also says in the Bible, 'Do not worry about tomorrow; tomorrow will take care of itself'" (Mt 6:34). With that, we left for home.

Shirley and I became friends that day. I cut a lot of wood for her that year, and we always took some time to share a prayer and some Scripture. She had a good sense of humor, and we laughed a lot. We were from different cultures and religious backgrounds, and she came at things from a totally different and interesting perspective. I sometimes wondered if she had ever spent much time outside of her home county. She would ask me some tough questions such as, "Brother Mark, what do you think about the thousand-year reign of Revelation 20?" Sometimes I just didn't know where to begin. She once asked me if I knew what the difference was between the Holy Ghost and the Holy Spirit. I knew that she was not just talking about different translations from the Greek, so I answered that I did not know. She said, "Well I was just thinkin' that the Holy Ghost is what you feel on the inside and the Holy Spirit is what you feel on the outside." I guess that some of our mystics have come up with some ideas that that are a lot farther out there than that over the years! One day I told Shirley that I would not be able to cut wood for a few days because I was going to fly up to New York to visit my grandmother. She answered, "Very well, child, but the only time I'm ever gonna' fly is when I fly to meet Jesus!"—an allusion to 1 Thessalonians 4:17. She taught me to be ready for spontaneous prayer, and, sometimes, when I arrived to cut wood, she would say, "Now is time for prayer; you lead out!"

Shirley and John have since made the passage to the other

side. They are gone in the physical sense but live on in the memories of those who knew them. *May they rest in peace.*

The last time I was in Hartford, I drove down Shirley's street and noticed that her small shack had been removed. The lot was totally bare, and all the cats were gone. There is now no trace of the humble home of a faithful Christian woman whose love of God's Word and whose absolute trust in God brought much light and joy to the heart of a young man discerning a vocation of service in Christ's Church.

I am grateful for those who have guided and inspired me along this journey.

Cutting wood for Shirley with fellow Glenmary candidate, Rob

CHAPTER 8

Daniel: The Virtue of Joy

A joyful heart is the health of the body, but a de-
pressed spirit dries up the bones.
—PROVERBS 17:22

As noted in the previous chapter, I was able to gain some invaluable experience in parish ministry and community service during my time as a Glenmary candidate. Among the places I volunteered was a workshop that employed physically and mentally challenged persons. I was assigned to assist some of the employees with their learning goals in such areas as basic math skills, reading, currency identification, and making change for a dollar. I also helped some employees with their workload, which primarily entailed cutting plastic tubing for automotive electrical parts and bagging plastic plumbing parts.

On my first day, Linda, one of the three supervisors, brought me around to meet the workers. They were all very nice to me, and many of them invited me to assist them in their tasks and to sit beside them right away. It is so nice to be wanted! One of the workers I met that day was Daniel, and I instantly knew that he was a very caring person. He had a bright smile as he steadily placed plumbing parts in small plastic bags. After I introduced myself, he immediately said with a smile, "It sure is a great day, isn't it?"

Linda shook her head and replied, "Daniel, it's a little early in the day for all that happiness." We all laughed.

Back in the office, Linda told me about some of the family histories of the workers. Special Education had not really been introduced into the school system in this area until recently, so many of those with special needs had only received a minimum of formal education, and some had hardly gone to school at all. I could not see any deficiency with Daniel's intellect, but he had some back and leg problems and was only able to walk slowly with the help of a special cane. His father had apparently been very protective and had not permitted Daniel to work outside of the home. In fact, I don't think that he had ever spent much time at all outside of the family abode.

Apparently, it was only after his father's death that Daniel, at the young age of sixty-four, was able to start his first job at this workshop. At an age when many are already retired, or at least short-timers, Daniel was looking forward to going to work each day. Each morning, he enthusiastically waited for the van that would pick him up in front of his home. He worked each day with a broad smile. I worked with Daniel some on that first day, and he told me with sincere pride, "Mark, I got my first pay-check last week. I made twelve dollars and thirty-seven cents."

His joy was genuine, and I was humbled upon hearing his words, which caused me to confront my own materialistic and greedy past. I recalled that, in my senior year of college in 1983, whenever I told fellow students and friends that I just had been offered a starting salary of $21,527 with the Department of the Navy, I was always quick to add that my salary would increase to $25,000 after six months, which did not include overtime. After I began full-time work, I had quite a wish list of world-ly items. Now, I don't mind giving things away, but it is very humbling to look back and see my own selfishness. Although, at the peak of my engineering career, I was making about twice the average household income, I never seemed to be able to save much money, and I was never very charitable in sharing much of my treasure with those less fortunate. I lived a self-centered existence with some isolation, and there were times when I was even embarrassed that I wasn't making more money.

I had just met Daniel, and I was sure that he would have given part or all of his meager paycheck to anyone in need. He knew that there were more important things than material pos-sessions, and he helped me with that insight. Daniel became a good friend during my time in Kentucky, and I always looked forward to seeing him on Wednesday mornings. He played his autoharp and guitar for the workshop Christmas party, and he even gave me a tape of some of the songs he had recorded. I still have that tape more than thirty years later, and I still remember Daniel's joy at the start of each workday. If more workers had his attitude, workplaces would certainly improve, and productivity would not be a problem.

Pope St. John Paul II's 1981 encyclical, *Laborem Exercens* (On Human Work), teaches that work builds up society and is fulfilling to human beings who are actually sharing in the activity of God our Creator. He also points out that the lives of disabled persons have the same dignity and sanctity as all others. For this reason, they should be allowed to participate in the life of society in all aspects and at all levels accessible to their capacities. Work is, therefore, not simply for economic advantage but is a participation in the building up of society.

Perhaps a machine could have been built to bag the plastic plumbing parts that Daniel so diligently bagged. That, however, would have been a great shame. Work can be fulfilling, especially when one takes pride in his or her work, whether it be in labor, management, or research. Society is indeed built up by faithful workers.

Thank you, Daniel, for showing me our human potential and your joy!

CHAPTER 9

The Revival in Pulaski

Do not worry beforehand of what you are to say.
But say whatever will be given you at that hour.
—MARK 13:11

" **N**ow you betta' be ready, cause there ain't no tellin' who I'm gonna' call on." His words were not threatening, but they were direct, and I took them seriously. It was a peaceful night in downtown Pulaski, Tennessee. I was working at a popcorn booth with a few parishioners from Immaculate Conception Catholic Church, which was the location of my novitiate with Glenmary. Pulaski has the unfortunate distinction of being the birthplace of the Ku Klux Klan, and, from time to time, Pulaski became the backdrop for bigots from different groups as a staging location for racist rallies and parades. In just a few days, the Arian Nations, a group with a message of hatred and violence, was planning to descend upon the peaceful downtown square in an attempt to garner media attention and increase support for their demented campaign.

Local church and civic leaders were opposed to the upcoming rally, and a grassroots campaign known as "Giles County United" was formed to promote a message of brotherhood, cooperation, and respect. On that particular night in the town square, there was much evidence of the good will that existed among the locals of Pulaski. The ministerial alliance had organized a night of Gospel singing, food, and fellowship. There was wide ecumenical participation and excellent attendance. Some congregations sold Bar-B-Que sandwiches, cold soft drinks, or hot dogs, while others had their choirs perform on a temporary stage. The small Catholic Parish of Immaculate Conception had been designated as the official popcorn providers for the evening.

Charlie Murphy, a friend of mine from the parish who was preparing to become a permanent deacon, and I had met in the square. At some point, we began to speak with an African American minister, Rev. Cornell Martin, who was the pastor of a small independent Baptist Church that had an excellent Gospel choir that had sung on the square that evening. During our conversation, Rev. Martin invited us to attend a week-long revival at their church, Ebenezer Baptist, which was set to begin in a few days. That is when he made the remark about "being ready." His invitation was sincere, but I think that he doubted that we would actually show up at the revival. As we were cleaning the popcorn machine at the end of the evening, I told Charley that we should go to the revival at least one night. He agreed and said that he knew where the church was, and we then made plans to meet. I kept wondering what I would say, if he did indeed "call" on me. This uncertainty was putting a large knot in my stomach.

Ebenezer Baptist was a small country church, and we arrived about ten minutes early. Several people were standing outside, and I admit that I was nervous when I saw their surprised looks as we pulled into the parking lot and got out of the car. With the history of racial tensions in Pulaski, I hoped that no one thought we were there to cause trouble. As we walked up, and they saw that I was carrying a Bible—a King James red-letter edition that I had checked out of the public library—I think they realized that we were indeed present for the revival. We were greeted warmly and, after entering the church, Charlie and I settled into the back pew. Pastor Martin was in the pulpit area with the guest evangelist, and he spotted us out of the corner of his eye. We weren't, of course, hard to pick out of the crowd! He smiled at us and said, "All ministers please come to the front." Charlie and I heard him, but we didn't move from our places. He then repeated his command from the microphone while pointing directly at us. Charlie and I slowly made our way to the seats directly behind the pulpit. I was pretty self-conscious about my position, but I tried to look relaxed. The congregation gradually settled down, and the service began.

The evangelist, Rev. Jerry Reeves, was truly an incredible speaker. He had the ability to mix and apply the words and message of Scripture to the problems of daily life in an interesting and often humorous way. I wish that I had been able to record his sermon for further reflection. He expounded on the vision of the bones from the thirty-seventh chapter of Ezekiel in a profound way. The basic thrust of his message was that our bones must be full of life that remains grounded in God. Rev. Reeves was a spirit filled man, and I admired him very much that night. During the sermon, the congregation interjected with exclamations such as, "Amen!" "Well?!" and "Fix it Up!" After his sermon, which was probably almost an hour long, he sat down and Rev. Martin turned to us, and then said to the congregation, "Now, we will hear from our visiting ministers." He turned and nodded to me.

I got up slowly and walked to the pulpit as I wondered what I could possibly say that would add anything to the fine message of the guest evangelist. I opened the Bible to the twenty-sixth chapter of Matthew and looked out. It was quiet, and I saw that everyone's eyes were on me. I softly said, "I was just thinking of Jesus in the Garden of Gethsemane when he asked Peter, James, and John to stay awake and pray. When he found them asleep, do you remember what he said? I opened the Bible and read with emphasis: "The Spirit is willing but the flesh is weak," and then commented, "And how true that is for us as well."

Some members of the congregation responded by proclaiming, "Amen," and then I went on to say something about how we often struggle against the weakness of the flesh but need to remain focused on the spiritual life. When I turned to return to my seat, a large woman in the choir exclaimed, "Well, he's all right!" That affirmation put me at ease and was much more than I had hoped for when I stepped up to the pulpit.

The revival concluded, and Charlie and I stayed around for a little while to speak with the evangelist, pastor, deacons, and some of the parishioners. We went back two nights later and again experienced an occasion of song, fellowship, and rejoicing in the Lord. Although I had attended Christian worship services outside of Catholic Church before this revival, I had never before been so moved by such an expression of faith. Experiences such as these have moved me to a greater ecumenical understanding.

While I am firmly grounded in Catholicism, I understand that all Christians share a common Baptism. I believe from such experiences that the Spirit of God can and does work outside of the visible boundaries of the Catholic Church. This point is stated in paragraph 3 of the "Decree on Ecumenism" of the Second Vatican Council:

> *The daily Christian life of these brethren is nourished by their faith in Christ and strengthened by the grace of Baptism and by hearing the word of God. This shows itself in their private prayer, their meditation on the Bible, in their Christian family life, and in the worship of a community gathered together to praise God. Moreover, their form of worship sometimes displays notable features of the liturgy which they shared with us of old.*

The revival in Pulaski affirmed for me that we are part of a greater family of Faith.

CHAPTER 10

Nancy Moore, An Unexpected Friend

*Faithful friends are a sturdy shelter; whoever finds
one finds a treasure.*
—SIRACH 6:14

Among the more memorable experiences during the mission phase of my novitiate in Fayetteville, Tennessee, with the Glenmary Home Missioners was the time when my supervisor, Fr. Tom Field, sent my brother novice, Keith, and me to serve in his place as chaplains of the week at the local hospital and its affiliated Skilled Care Center. This position rotated among the active ministers of the Lincoln County Ministerial Association, and the responsibilities included visiting the patients of the hospital of one's own denomination and those who listed "none" under the denominational affiliation. Claiming no church does not exempt one from the reach of pastoral care! The second part of the chaplaincy was presiding at a short Christian worship service in the lobby/activity room of the Skilled Care Center. Keith asked me if I would plan the worship service, and I agreed.

I thought that the easiest thing to do would be to sing a couple of hymns, have a short reading from the Gospel, and then a short reflection on Christmas, which was just a few weeks away. When the day came, we picked up the hospital printout and split up the few patients that we were to visit. After these visits, we went over to the Skilled Care Center for the Sunday devotional service.

When we arrived, the scene in the main lobby was one of total confusion. There were family members coming in for visits, there were people leaving, and many people were just standing around talking. I found someone who worked there and informed her that we were present for the Sunday service. She said that she would try to find the hymnals for us. As she went to the office to search for them, I looked around at the confusion, and I cynically thought that the whole thing was certainly not going to amount to much. The staff person returned with a few hymnals and then attempted to inform the residents and guests that the Sunday worship service was ready to begin.

As she was talking, I noticed a quiet and nicely dressed woman in a wheelchair with her Bible across her lap. She was about the only one who appeared to be patiently awaiting the start of our worship service. I walked over and jokingly asked her if she was going to "bring the Word" to us today, but she took me seriously and replied, "No, I reckon' you are, preacher." Now, up until that morning, I had been called many things, but I'll never forget that moment when I was first called "preacher." It accentuated for me an awareness of the importance of breaking open the Word of God.

A few people gathered around while others continued to talk in other parts of the room. We introduced ourselves and then began our service with Amazing Grace. I read from the Gospel of Luke then talked about the love of God and the humility of our Lord who was born in a palace, right? "No preacher," the quiet woman replied, "He was born in a stable." I smiled at her, and she smiled back. After we concluded with our final hymn, I asked her what her name was, and if it would be all right if I visited her. She told me that her name was Nancy Moore, and that she would like for me to visit anytime.

A few days later, I went over and hoped that she would remember me. She did, and I spent about an hour talking to her and her roommate, Miss Pearle. They had both grown up in rural hollows of Tennessee, and they shared lots of stories of growing up in what most people of my generation would consider primitive conditions. They also talked of their faith, their families, and life in general. I was so impressed with them that I went by to visit every few days and spent a lot of time with them. There was a real chemistry between these two women of a different generation and culture and myself. Someone in the parish had given me a starter mix for some Amish friendship bread, and I baked a loaf for these new friends of mine. They really seemed to appreciate it.

The mission phase of my novitiate was rapidly coming to a close, and I would soon be moving to Cincinnati. Since we were just beginning to get to know one another and enjoyed the time that we spent together, I dreaded telling my new friends of my upcoming move. When I finally told them, Nancy asked me if there was any way that I could stay in Lincoln County. She said that she really liked our visits. I tried to explain that I had to continue my ministerial studies, but I also promised that I would be back to visit when I could.

Shortly after going to Cincinnati for the discernment stage of my novitiate, I discontinued my formation and studies with Glenmary and moved home to North Carolina. In the one and a half years that I was affiliated with Glenmary, I visited a lot of nursing home residents and home-bound people. At the time, my parents were in fairly good health, but I began to wonder what it would be like if one of them was in a nursing home and I was 400 or 500 miles away. If I was a priest for the Diocese of Charlotte, I would always be fairly close to home and able to visit my parents every week. After some time of prayer, I disaffiliated with Glenmary and applied to the seminarian program for my home diocese of Charlotte. Fortunately, I was accepted and, as before, I did not have a "Plan B."

Seven months later, I traveled from North Carolina to visit those friends that I had made in Kentucky and Tennessee during my time there. Of course, I went by the Skill Center to visit Miss Nancy and Miss Pearle. As I approached the room, I got an empty feeling when I noticed that Nancy's name was not on the door and there was a different person in her bed. Thinking the worst, I slowly asked Miss Pearle, who at ninety-three still looked fine, if Nancy had moved. She answered that Nancy had slipped and broken her hip, and that she had been moved upstairs for rehabilitation.

I found her new room, and I saw that she was lying in the bed trembling in pain. It was difficult to see my friend suffering so much. Her eyes were closed when I asked her how she was doing. She recognized my voice and said, "Mark, is that you?"

"Yes, Nancy, it is. I've come to see you," I replied.

She extended her shaking hand, and I held it. She tried to apologize for her condition, and I told her that she certainly went to a lot of trouble to get more attention. She laughed, and I cried. I prayed that the Lord would grant her peace, healing, and an end to her suffering. She thanked me and then said, "I didn't know if I would ever see you again." That was to be our last meeting on this earth. Very soon thereafter, she passed beyond the physical pain of her crippled body. She is, however, not forgotten, and I look forward to seeing her again in our Father's house.

She was an unexpected friend who enriched my life.

CHAPTER 11

Sr. Angela Frances: My "Unofficial" Spiritual Director

The spiritual person, however, can judge everything
but is not subject to judgment by anyone.
—1 COR. 2:15

One of the challenges of my religious formation was the "directed retreat." You may know that seminarians are required to make at least one retreat every year. For those of you who have never made a directed retreat, I'll provide a brief summary based solely on my own experiences. A directed retreat for a seminarian usually occurs away from the seminary at a retreat center. The typical length of a retreat is about a week, and part of each day is spent meeting with a spiritual director. The challenge for me was relating well with the spiritual director at the retreat center who may not have been the person I would have chosen. When one has a difficult situation with a retreat director, it becomes an additional burden added to an already challenging retreat. As a seminarian, I never wanted anything negative to be included in my folder as I hoped that I would be accepted for ordination. There is a key difference between a directed retreat for a seminarian and a retreat for a lay person. The seminarian has to continue the requirements of the seminary. A lay person may simply leave and go home, or tell the director, "We're done," if he or she is not enjoying the retreat.

I believe that most spiritual directors sincerely intend to help the retreatant by providing some insights about one's spiritual or personal life. It has been my experience, however, that mixed in with such helpful insights is a projection from his or her own spiritual life or challenges. Some spiritual directors, for example, do not seem to be able to resist recommending their favorite books, voicing their opinions and perspectives on the state of the Church or the world, or both, and trying to implement a little psychology.

I think that the concept of having a type of "spiritual guru" to guide one along the spiritual journey and to facilitate one's self-awareness is a worthy one, and I am certainly in favor of all people making retreats. In fact, the idea of a spiritual mentor reminds me of the wise older monks who asked thought-provoking questions and gave advice to the young "Grasshopper" on the old "Kung Fu" television series, which I enjoyed in my youth. The problem for me has been connecting well with an "official" spiritual director on a retreat. However, I'll accept my part of the responsibility for this since I have been just as stubborn as any of the retreat masters that I've met. While there is always hope for a positive spiritual experience on retreats, this story is an account of what happened to me on a retreat when I felt trapped with my assigned spiritual director. Somehow, by the grace of God, it all worked out for the best.

Fr. Gilead told me during our first session, "Now Mark, I don't have an agenda. This is your retreat, and we'll let the Holy Spirit do the guiding." Well, that was what he said, but as I left the room after the first of our nine meetings, I thought that, perhaps, he did have an agenda whether he was aware of it or not. This particular director is a fine man and a scholarly priest and professor, but we just did not connect in this setting. In fact, I really didn't look forward to our daily sessions but simply wrote it off as one of the burdens of religious formation.

This particular retreat took place in my second year at St. Meinrad Seminary at the retreat house of the Sisters of Charity of Nazareth in their motherhouse complex near Bardstown, Kentucky. Our class was asked to refrain from all talking except during our community conference sessions, during our daily celebration of the Eucharist, and, of course, during the sessions with our directors for the entire nine days.

I had been to Nazareth once before, and I really liked the place and the grounds. I asked one of the sisters there on my previous visit, "Sister what are y'all doing with those white buildings at the end of that large field?"

She smiled and said, "Well, they don't belong to us. That is part of the Jim Beam Distillery where they make Kentucky bourbon." Okay, interesting neighbors!

Another time, I was looking out the window toward the cemetery, and I could see hundreds of simple white crosses marking the graves of the many sisters who had died since their foundation about 150 years earlier. At the entrance to the cemetery, there were seven or eight giant mausoleums containing the earthly remains of their former chaplains. There was such a contrast between the simple markers for the sisters and the granite monstrosities for the priests. Another sister was also looking out the window at the light snowfall, and I said, "Sister, it looks as though clericalism goes to the grave."

She responded with a smile and said, "The glories of this world are transitory" (see 2 Cor 4:18).

In Nazareth, I enjoyed praying in the French gothic chapel of the motherhouse, which is very beautiful. On one of the first mornings of the retreat, I was reading my Bible in this chapel and a short elderly nun approached me and said, "Are you the one that asked me about my rosary?"

I was a bit confused by her question since I had not spoken to anyone on the premises. I was sure that she had me mixed up with someone else, so I answered, "No, Sister. That must have been someone else."

She then asked where I was from, and I told her that I was a seminarian studying at St. Meinrad for the Diocese of Charlotte, North Carolina. With a beautiful smile, she said, "That's great, we need you!" She introduced herself as Sr. Angela Frances.

Our conversation continued, and I think that we were the only ones in the chapel at the time. The supreme silence that I had been asked to observe was totally shattered. She showed me around the church and explained each of the beautiful stained-glass windows, and she told me of the past renovations, including the one when she was a young sister in about 1922. She shared with me her love for the poor and the underprivileged and told me of her work in the field of education in the "missions." She pointed out an old and unused brick building near the motherhouse where she and the other novices had once spent long hours hand washing the bed linens and towels for the prep school more than seventy years earlier.

I was in awe of her sense of peace and serenity, and I tried to picture the motherhouse of Nazareth, Kentucky, of the past with its school, farm, and hired workers. I attempted to visualize this now senior nun as a teenager arriving after the ten-mile trip to the motherhouse from her family farm in a horse drawn carriage with her parents. Her religious vocation had not grown sour over the many years, nor had she become cynical or grouchy as others have. She truly lived the virtues of hospitality, prayer, and faithfulness. On that first morning, Sr. Angela Frances introduced me to the cook, the housekeeping staff, the sisters serving in administration, and the sister who served as the sacristan. We sat down and chatted over cookies and coffee, and, when I looked at my watch, I realized that I had about one minute to make it to the 11:15 am Mass on the third floor of the retreat building, which was about a quarter of a mile up the road. I told Sr. Angela Frances that I had to leave but that I would see her again. I ran up the road full speed, up the steps as there was no elevator, and down the hall. With our small class, I knew that I would be missed. They had waited for me, and, as I tried to slip into the room that served as our chapel, I was so winded that I was unable to sing the opening hymn.

Throughout the week, I met with Sr. Angela Frances every day, often over coffee and cookies. We talked of faith, virtue, and ministry, and she showed me more of the motherhouse, including Heritage Hall, the basement of the chapel, the liturgical storage room, and even the mailroom. I introduced her to one of my classmates, so I guess I was guilty of fostering the non-silent behavior of another. As the retreat continued, I managed to endure the daily sessions with my assigned spiritual director, but, upon reflection, I know that I was very fortunate to have become aquatinted with a very special servant of God.

Doing the Lord's work in a spirit of humility with a good sense of humor were among the qualities that I really admired in Sr. Angela Frances. I still chuckle when I think of some of her stories. One that I really liked was her description of one of their former chaplains, an Irish priest who had a trusty dog that followed him everywhere including the confessional. On one occasion, the Mother Superior apparently let their dear chaplain know that she objected to this, and that she would not confess her sins in the presence of his canine friend. The priest apparently replied, "Mother, go ahead and make your confession. This dog is bound to the same seal of the sacrament as is his master."

Although in her nineties, Sr. Angela Frances was discouraged that she wasn't given more to do. She told me that the word "retirement" should be banished from the English language, and that some of their "retired" sisters could now be doing the best work of their lives. After that retreat, Sr. Angela Frances and I wrote to each other a few times, and I stopped in to visit her at Nazareth a couple of times either on my way home to North Carolina or on the trip back to the seminary. She eventually moved to the Nazareth Home for retired sisters in Louisville where she passed seventy-five years of professed religious life. The last time that I saw her, she had slipped a little mentally, and her memory was not as sharp, but she still had her warm smile and that friendly disposition of Christian hospitality and charity.

I was certainly fortunate to have her as a friend, and as an "unofficial" spiritual director.

Sister Angela Frances

CHAPTER 12

Hospital Chaplaincy: Portraits of Faith

*Peter said, "I have neither silver nor gold, but what
I do have I give you: in the name of Jesus Christ the
Nazorean, rise and walk."
Then Peter took him by the right hand and raised
him up, and immediately his feet and ankles grew
strong. He leaped up, stood, and walked around,
and went into the temple with them, walking and
jumping and praising God.*
—ACTS 3:6-8

In my seminary program, one summer was designated for Clinical Pastoral Education (CPE). Certification in this field was required for the Master of Divinity degree. I was fortunate in that I was approved to complete this ecumenical hospital chaplaincy in the lovely city of Charleston at Bon Secours St. Francis Hospital. During the summer, I was blessed to live in the beautiful parish of Stella Maris on Sullivan's Island with Msgr. McInerny, a priest that I had known since 1985 (see Chapter 5). CPE is known to be a challenging and sometimes stressful experience. I figured that if I had to do it, I might as well try to do it in a beautiful place where I still had some good friends. Sitting on the front porch of the rectory in the evening looking at the Charleston harbor was also a great experience— in addition to the opportunities to go cycling, boating, and fishing!

In those days, CPE relied heavily on psychology. There seemed to be two questions that were asked in various ways to the student chaplains over the course of the ten-week program.

The first was: "Are you in touch with your pain?" The follow-up question was: "Are you in touch with your anger?" We were tasked to minister to patients in the hospital and, the hope was that we would grow in spirituality and self-knowledge in the process. There is sometimes a reluctance in human nature to be around those who are suffering. Perhaps this calls to mind one's own mortality and the fragility of life. There may even be a sense of guilt if one is in fine health and another person has multiple health concerns. My experiences among the suffering have included this reluctance, and yet, more powerfully, I've experienced moments of grace and faith. I think that the concept of CPE is a good one. The problem is that it is not always carried out in a healthy way. I heard of a case in which a student chaplain actually attacked a supervisor after a consistent and unjust critique of his pastoral visits. The supervisors even invited us to join in their world, and, in one our conferences, a supervisor said to us, "You are protecting each other. Don't hesitate to challenge each other!"

The supervisors were certainly experienced in probing young chaplains as we related our experiences with the patients. Including myself, we had five chaplains in our group. My supervisor had the title Protestant Chaplain. We went through an orientation and were then assigned to various floors of the hospital for pastoral care. I was assigned to the oncology floor. I admit that when I was given my assignment, I did not know what the word meant. I was just told that there were some very ill people on that floor. Overall, I enjoyed visiting the patients.

Our chaplain conferences were called Group Dynamics, and, in these, we were tasked to relate our pastoral visits. One of my fellow student chaplains was a Methodist pastor who was completing his seminary training. During one group session, he explained that he just visited a man with leukemia, but that the patient did not have much to share with him. The Protestant Chaplain saw this as an opportunity to poke a little to see if he could prompt a reaction. He asked him, "Did that man remind you of your father?"

The chaplain was genuinely shocked at the question and

shook his head as he replied, "No."

The supervisor continued, "Your father is an alcoholic, isn't he?"

The chaplain said, "What?"

The supervisor added, "You really hate your father, don't you?"

I saw this as an unreasonable line of questions as we had heard nothing in his description of his pastoral visit that had anything to do with his relationship to his father. It was just a basic visit. Having already had some experiences in the seminary with directed retreats, spiritual direction, psychology, and yearly evaluations, I was determined not to let the supervisors get to me. It was a challenge, though, because they were well trained in this enterprise. Despite my resolve to take everything in stride, I did insult the supervisors indirectly a couple of times during Group Dynamics.

Towards the end of the summer, my vocation director (seminarian supervisor), Fr. Frank called me from Charlotte and asked, "Mark, how is it going?"

I replied, "I don't think that I will receive a very good evaluation as I have fought with them a little."

He encouraged, "Just get in a good cry in the group session before the end of the summer, and all will be well." That remark made me smile, and I did manage to pass the course.

Several patient visits of that summer still stand out after all these years. I remember visiting a retired pastor. He was African American and was raised in a small community outside of Charleston. In addition to being a minister at Daydawn Baptist Church, he had worked in many manual labor jobs. He had dark skin and gray hair, and I can remember being inspired by his faith and his outlook. He was a sincere believer, and, when he mentioned that he was waiting for the Lord, I asked him, "What has the Lord been saying to you?"

He responded, "He's preparing my place. I'm living on the side of the mountain, but my home is on the mountaintop with Jesus—for He said, 'I am going to prepare a place for you, so that where I am, you also may be' (Jn 14:3). I might go to sleep and wake up on the other side. We don't know when we will go home to the Lord. I have run the race and kept the faith."

He then gave me some pastoral advice: "Stay on the King's highway. There may be curves, hills, and bends, but stay on the road. And we'll meet together in the household of the Lord above the moon, the sun, and the stars—above sickness and suffering—above pain and death." These were sincere words of faith and trust in Divine Providence. It was a true example of the patient ministering to the chaplain.

On another visit on the oncology floor, I visited a patient in a darkened room. The blinds were closed, and the door was partially open. The female patient was speaking, and I initially thought that she was speaking with someone in the room. I then realized that she was speaking to God in a very intense tone. Her words reminded me of the lament that we find in Psalm 130 regarding the reality of human suffering: "Out of the depths I call to you, Lord; Lord, hear my cry!" (Ps 130:1–2). I could hear her say, "I will not suffer any more. Why should I? You know me. This is my last day of suffering."

I knocked on the door and entered. She looked over to me and said, "Yes, doctor?"

I replied, "No, I'm not the doctor. I'm the chaplain for this floor."

She extended her hand and said, "Please, come here." She firmly grasped my hand and closed her eyes, and then said with great passion, "Only you have the blueprint, Lord; Only you have the contract. This is the last day of my suffering. Why should I serve a God who does not hear me? See this man. This is no ordinary man. He is one of your chosen ones. He is one of your own. You said that when two are gathered together in your name, you hear their prayer. Bring me to glory or heal me. You made this piece of junk; you are the only one who can help. These doctors do not have the blueprint. This is the last day of my suffering. Bring me to glory or heal me. Listen to me and to your chosen one here for we are joined in prayer."

I was bit overwhelmed with her intense prayer, but then I remembered the above passage from the Acts of the Apostles when St. Peter prayed for the healing of the crippled man out-side the temple. I prayed, "Lord, I pray for an end to this illness and an increase in strength. In the name of Jesus, I pray that she be healed."

After a long pause, she opened her eyes and looked at me. She was suddenly calm. In a normal voice, she said, "I'm fine now. The Lord is never late. He sent you here at the right time. He doesn't always do what you want Him to do, but He is never late. He sent you here for a purpose. I'm going to be all right. The Lord has the blueprint, and He will enlighten the minds of the doctors. I will be well soon. This is my last day of suffering. It was you He sent. No other believer has been here today." Her final words were, "Keep doing the Lord's work, and let Him guide you. I will be fine."

That pastoral visit of twenty-eight years ago is still fresh in my mind. While I can't even explain exactly what her medical condition was or her treatments or what actually happened, I am able say that she recovered and went home a day or two later. When I related this pastoral visit in our group session, I remember my supervisor, the Protestant Chaplain, being some-what skeptical that anything significant had taken place. He would sometimes question faith almost as if he were an agnos-tic. He sarcastically said, "Mark, I would not recommend open-ing a healing ministry on the fourth floor." It was a unique visit, and it remains humbling for me to imagine that I may be used as an instrument of healing in the Divine Plan. It also affirmed for me the power of prayer.

Yes, I believe in miracles.

Another inspiring patient from that summer was the late Harry Smalls. Harry was a tall, slim African American man with very clear eyes. He was seventy-seven years old and was very ill from cancer and the related complications. When I first met him, he still had his hair, which was short and gray. He was the type of person who never complained even though he was often uncomfortable with all of his treatments and IV's. When I introduced myself as the chaplain of the floor, he invit-ed me in with a sincere smile. I asked him how he was, and he replied that he wasn't well, but that he was sure that the Lord wouldn't put more on him then he could take. This became a familiar quote that he said from his heart. It reminded me of the words of St. Paul to the struggling Christian community at Corinth: "God is faithful and will not let you be tried beyond your strength; but with the trial he will also provide a way out, so that you may be able to bear it" (1 Cor 10:13). Harry seemed at peace with his suffering, although he was hardly overjoyed by it.

In the beginning of my summer course, I looked forward to visiting Harry because he was easy to visit, and, thus, it was a secure and safe environment for me. Some patients on the oncology floor where I had been assigned were very troubled, confused, or even bitter, and the visits were at times challenging, awkward, or even hostile. As the time went on, however, I developed a friendship with Harry. He ministered to me as I tried to minister to him. He had a great love for Sacred Scripture—God's inspired Word. He often greeted me by saying, "Okay, you got a Scripture for me today?" After picking several passages over the first few weeks, I finally asked him if there was something that he would like to hear. He mentioned that his favorite Psalm was Psalm 27, which begins: "The Lord is my light and my salvation; whom should I fear? The Lord is my life's refuge; of whom should I be afraid?"

Although I was familiar with this psalm from the Liturgy of the Hours and the Mass, the words took on a special meaning for me as I read them to a suffering man of faith who was near the end of his earthly pilgrimage.

During my visits, Harry shared much of his life with me. He had worked about fifty years as a handyman and general house servant for a well-to-do man. I could tell that he was a man of integrity and decency and was surely trusted by his long-time employer. His wife visited every day with a mentally handicapped niece. They prayed and trusted in God while Harry's health continued to decline. He told me several times that he was waiting on the Lord. The words of his favorite psalm encouraged him: "Wait for the Lord, take courage; be stout-hearted, wait for the Lord" (Ps 27:14).

Near the end of my course, Harry was moved to the Intensive Care Unit. I asked a nurse if she thought that Harry would ever be released from the hospital, and she answered that she didn't think he would be leaving through the front door. Although he was heavily sedated, I think that Harry could hear me as I visited him for the last time. I prayed for him, and I knew that our heavenly Father had a special place for him. I then prayed with his wife and niece in the ICU waiting room. They seemed to appreciate my concern.

One week after I was back at the seminary, Harry's wait came to end, and he went to meet the Lord. His life had a major impact on me, and, when I think of Harry, I'm grateful to have known him. He remains a friend in my heart and through his last ten weeks, I was shown a living portrait of faith and trust.

I think of him often especially during the Liturgy of the Hours when the universal Church prays Psalm 27. On my ordination card, I included the following verse of that Psalm in memory of a faithful man who showed me what the words truly mean:

One thing I ask of the Lord; this I seek:
To dwell in the Lord's house all the days of my life.
—PSALM 27:4

CHAPTER 13

Katie, My Prayer Partner

For where two or three are gathered together in my
name, there am I in the midst of them.
—MT. 18:20

The course of studies for a priesthood candidate is a very structured curriculum, which to some degree has essentially been in place for hundreds of years. There are, however, a few options that a seminarian may decide for himself, and I always tried to make the most of those opportunities. For example, one does have a few academic electives and the opportunity to do a self-initiated study during the January interterm. I was also able to choose the retreat center for three of my required retreats. For the retreat preceding my ordination to the diaconate, I was inspired to go to the Tampa Bay area of Florida. This really is true! It turned out to be one of my better inspirations, and this retreat is the backdrop for the following story.

I had left the Franciscan retreat center on Saturday morning to look for the cathedral of the Diocese of St. Petersburg where I planned to pray the morning office of the Liturgy of the Hours. I then intended to either walk or bike along the bay road and enjoy the view. I didn't know the city, and I didn't have a city map. This happened well before cell phones and GPS. I thought that I might just get lucky and come upon the cathedral as I drove around town. Sometimes, the Catholic cathedral is right in the heart of the city and easy to find.

Well, I drove in circles around St. Petersburg for quite a while with no success. I admit that I didn't stop anywhere to ask, but I guess that I inherited that trait from my father. After much time and many miles, I finally saw a Catholic parish, and I thought, *Well it's not the cathedral, but it will be fine for my morning prayers.* I parked my car and then soon discovered that the church was locked and there was no one in sight. I then had a change of plans. Since the morning was already half over, I would simply pray the morning office in the nearby park that overlooked the beautiful Tampa Bay.

It was a pleasant morning, and I found an empty bench in the park. I noticed a young woman sitting on the sea wall about thirty yards in front of me who was looking over the bay while listening to a portable radio with headphones. I began to pray in this peaceful location with a fresh breeze in my face. As I made the Sign of the Cross at the start of the Canticle of Zechariah, I happened to look up and noticed that the woman who had been sitting on the sea wall was now lying on the grass and watching me very carefully. You might say that she was staring at me. I again focused my attention on my prayers and, as I began to do the intercessions from my prayer book, I again looked up and noticed that she was now standing right beside me. I was a little startled and unsure of what to expect. She looked to be about eighteen, but her face was childlike. She was a little heavy and she was wearing sweatpants and still had the headphones on her head. We exchanged the following dialog:

She asked in a soft voice, "Are you praying?"

"Yes, I am," I replied.

She continued, "I'm sorry to bother you, but I just wanted you to know that I was praying with you. I love Jesus, and I'm not prejudiced. I love all types of people."

I responded, "That's great to hear. I don't know what I would do without the Lord Jesus in my life."

"Is that a Bible?" she asked as she pointed to my Breviary.

"This is my prayer book, which has parts of the Bible in it along with other prayers," I explained.

"That's nice. What Church do you go to?" she continued.

"I go to the Catholic Church."

"That one down the street?" she said as she motioned in the direction of the locked church that I had found.

"No, I'm from North Carolina," I said with a smile.

"North Carolina? You sure did come a long way."

"Yes, but I'm glad that I came. It's nice here."

"When I saw you do this (she attempted to make the Sign of the Cross), I thought that you were praying, so I just wanted you to know that I was praying with you. We should support one another. I just came out for some fresh air. I just live down the street. What is your name so that I can continue to pray for you?"

"I'm Mark (as I extended my hand), and your name?"

"Katie. May the Lord bless you."

"Thanks so much, and may He bless you and keep you safe." Katie then turned, walked off and waved.

Katie was one whom some would categorize as mentally handicapped or slow. The truth is that she is definitely not spiritually handicapped. She has a deep love for the Lord and a peaceful disposition. She taught me something about faith sharing. She was not intrusive; she was not demanding but very gentle.

As I finished my morning prayers, I looked out across the bay and reflected on Katie, my new prayer partner, and my sister in the Family of God.

As I enjoyed the scenic view, it didn't bother me that I had missed the cathedral and that the parish church was locked.

CHAPTER 14

Henry: A Man of Troubles

*[At the tomb of Lazarus,] Jesus told her, "I am the
resurrection and the life;
whoever believes in me, even if he dies, will
live, and everyone who lives
and believes in me will never die.
Do you believe this?"*
—JOHN 11:25–26

"**C**haplain, Chaplain, could you come here for a minute?" I looked around and saw a man quickly moving toward me, and I quickly deduced that he was calling me. I was spending my last summer as a seminarian at a parish in Belmont, North Carolina, and I had just visited an ill parishioner in the hospital in nearby Gastonia. When I heard the man's call, I was actually thinking about where I was going to go for lunch.

My first reaction was that since I was wearing a clerical collar, the man must have concluded that I was a chaplain of the hospital. "Yes?" I responded.

Coming up to me, he said, "My father has just had a serious stroke, and the whole family is going bonkers. Would you come up and talk to them?"

"Yes, of course I will." I said this with a lot more confidence than I felt. Although I had completed an intensive course in hospital chaplaincy, these situations are never routine, but I could not refuse a sincere call for help. I did not know if I could be of any assistance, but I was willing to try.

I followed the man to the elevator, and we went together to

the waiting room for the Intensive Care Unit. On the way, he said, "Our minister will not come, but that is another story." I deduced that there was some history there but decided that it was not the time to ask for an explanation.

In the waiting room there were four or five tall and lean men and a few women. The men were wearing tee-shirts, and their arms displayed various tattoos. I wasn't sure of all the family relationships. The man who had called me was older than the others and was well dressed, and he seemed to be a little out of place with the others. I deduced that he was the oldest son.

He introduced me to his sister who was crying. She looked at me and said, "We are worried about his soul. He has always said that he doesn't believe in God. Now he has had a massive stroke and is in critical condition. He is not able to respond. We're trying to get one of our brothers released from prison in Raleigh to come and see him."

A younger woman approached crying profusely and exclaimed, "What are we going to do? What are we going to do?"

The other men were standing around very quietly, and I didn't know what to say. After a quiet pause, I asked if he was alert. They responded by saying that he had been earlier. I then asked if we could see him. The oldest daughter told me to follow her.

About four of the family members and I went to his room in the ICU. In the bed, I saw a man fighting for his life with all that he had. He was also a lean man with long hair and a long gray beard. He was breathing with the assistance of an oxygen mask and had a number of IVs in his arm. As we gathered around the bed, his eyes met the eyes of his family members, and then he put his gaze on me, an outsider to the family with a shirt that represented ministry.

The younger lady, perhaps a daughter-in-law, still crying, cried out, "We need you, Dad. We need you."

She was on my left, and I asked her for his name. She told me, "His name is Henry."

After a period of silence, I looked into Henry's eyes and asked, "Henry, is it okay if we have a prayer?"

He looked back, and, after a moment, he slightly nodded his head up and down. I wouldn't say that I saw fear in his eyes, but I'm sure that he understood the severity of his physical condition, and he was surely concerned. Perhaps at that moment, he also saw his need for God's saving grace.

I opened my Bible to Matthew 11:28–30 and read some of the most comforting words of Scripture: "Come to me, all you who labor and are burdened, and I will give you rest. Take my yoke upon you and learn from me, for I am meek and humble of heart; and you will find rest for yourselves. For my yoke is easy, and my burden light." I paused to let the words sink in, and then I turned to John 6:35 and read: "Jesus said to them, 'I am the bread of life; whoever comes to me will never hunger, and whoever believes in me will never thirst.'"

I remained focused on Henry, and I felt as though the Word of God had touched him. I continued, "Henry, turn to Jesus, and put all your cares in his hands. Our Lord came and died for our sins, and He will never abandon us in our time of need. Henry, I pray in the name of Jesus that you will know his healing touch and that you will be given every grace needed to face this challenge. I pray for your family gathered here and for all the others that God will keep all of you in the palm of his hand on this day and for all the days of your life. May God's peace be with you."

His eyes were weary, bearing evidence of the strain of the fight. After a period of silence, we left the room and talked briefly in the hall. I assured them of my continued prayers.

The following couple of days were busy in the parish, but I continued to think about Henry and his family. A few days later, I was back at the hospital to visit our parishioner, and I returned to the Intensive Care Unit. I did not see any of Henry's family in the waiting room, so I went into the unit, and, upon entering, I saw that Henry's cubicle was empty. I asked the nurse at the desk where the patient was who had been in that space a few days earlier.

She inquired, "Are you family?"

I answered that I was not, but that I had visited him once.

She stated that she remembered seeing me with his family and that Henry had expired shortly afterwards. His physical struggle had ended.

Initially, Henry's daughter told me that she was worried about his soul. When I left the hospital that day, I knew that his life was in God's hands. I believe in the greatness of God's love and mercy, and while I know nothing about the eternal judgment of this man or any person (other than the saints), I have faith in a God who "wills everyone to be saved and to come to the knowledge of the truth" (1 Tm 2:4). Scripture tells us that "the Lord is gracious and merciful, slow to anger and abounding in mercy" (Ps 145:8).

Was I sent to Henry's side to bring God's inspired words in his final moments? Was I sent to speak of the love and sacrifice of Jesus to a searching soul? I do not claim to understand the ways of God, and it is humbling to think that almighty God may use me in His plan.

On my way to lunch one day, a man called out to me as a chaplain because I was wearing a black shirt with a white tab and carrying a Bible. It is humbling to think that my help was requested simply based on what I was wearing and what I was carrying. I know that what is truly important is who I represent and that only by being a person of prayer and trust will I be worthy of this calling.

Part of ministry is being open to the unexpected.

CHAPTER 15

The Eternal City of Rome

*Paul, a slave of Christ Jesus, called to be an apostle
and set apart for the Gospel of God . . .
to all the beloved of God in Rome, called to be holy.
Grace to you and peace from God our Father and
the Lord Jesus Christ.*
—ROMANS 1:1 & 7

I have had the great fortune of visiting Rome on three occasions. I first went as a seminarian in 1993 with a group
from St Meinrad Seminary. I returned as a young priest to
concelebrate the diaconate ordination of a friend in St. Peter's
Basilica in 1996 and then as part of the delegation of the Pontifical Mission Societies of the United States in 2013 when I
was serving on the Board of Directors.

I can remember well my first experience in Rome. As I stood
in the elliptical piazza of St. Peter's Basilica that night, I was caught
up in the moment. I had just arrived in the "Eternal City," and it
was a peaceful and mild night. As I took in the impressive view
of the basilica with its great dome, the statues, the fountains, and
the columns, I began to forget the challenges and frustrations of
the previous twenty-four hours, which included canceled flights,
a closed airport, long layovers, and lost luggage. Even though I
was feeling the fatigue of travel, I was in awe as I stood in silent
wonder in front of the steps of the most famous church in Christendom—a church that had begun as a small memorial erected
by persecuted Christians over the martyred remains of St. Peter,
the Galilean fisherman who became the first Bishop of Rome.

Officially, I had come to Rome as a student. Thirteen of

us from St. Meinrad Seminary had come to learn about Christian art and architecture for about two weeks. I had decided to meet our group in Rome and had, therefore, faced a number of travel challenges by myself. During our January interterm course, we were tasked with keeping a journal and reflecting on the theology and vision that shaped the different styles of the churches we visited. It was all very interesting, but, in my heart, I was a simple pilgrim. I always tried to remember that these are sacred places, not simply places to study. Many churches were built over places of martyrdom, and most churches house the physical remains of saints, the heroes and heroines of our Faith. These saints looked beyond the visible world to eternal life in peace in the Kingdom of God. Our faith is built on the faith of the saints.

Rome can be a very formative place for Christians. There are many relics in Rome, which remind us of a time of persecutions and serve as a connection with those who have gone before us. For example, the chains that bound St. Peter remind us of the potential consequences for following Christ and that fidelity to the Gospel entails making sacrifices. We are inspired by those who went before us and remained faithful. And, as Tertullian observed, the "blood of the martyrs is the seed of the Church."

Within the ancient city of Rome lies the Vatican City, the smallest sovereign state in the world with an area of only about 110 acres and a population of about 900. Its importance, however, goes far beyond these meager numbers. The pope is the head of state of the Vatican, but, more importantly, he is the Bishop of Rome and the successor of St. Peter to whom the Lord entrusted the "keys to the kingdom" (Mt 16:19). As successor of St. Peter, the pope has the burden and the responsibility of teaching and shepherding the flock of Christ. I like to think of the pope as our leading pastor.

I experienced a great sense of the universality of the Church in that first trip to Rome. On the feast of the Epiphany, I had the privilege of attending the ordination Mass of thirteen men to the episcopacy. The ordination took place in St. Peter's Basilica, and Pope St. John Paul II conferred the sacrament. The thirteen men who became bishops that day represented thirteen different countries and four continents, and all would serve in mission dioceses. The liturgy was celebrated in several different languages, which was a great reflection of the diversity of the Church and yet our unity with the successor of St. Peter and the Gospel message. Catholic means universal. There are many cultures, yet only one Faith. St. Peter's was filled to capacity on that joyous occasion, and it was clear to me that I was part of something greater than some human invention or institution. The Church is the Body of Christ (see 1 Cor 12:27), and, as we are united with Christ, we are also related to all of our brothers and sisters in the Lord.

That first trip to the "Eternal City" left a lasting impression on me. Three years later, I would again have a similar experience as I presented the grandeur of St. Peter's to my younger brother, Eric. We visited many places in Rome but kept returning to St. Peter's. On that trip, I concelebrated a Mass for a diaconate ordination in the basilica with about 300 other priests. That was such a memorable experience as a priest. Eric and I also prayed the Rosary with Pope St. John Paul II (and a couple of thousand others too!), so I can honestly say that I prayed the Rosary with a saint.

In 2013, on my last trip to Rome, I was part of a delegation organized by the Pontifical Mission Societies of the United States. As a member of the National Board, I was invited to participate in this *ad limina* visit. The United States is the largest contributor to the Church's missions, and so we were treated well during our visits to various Vatican offices, congregations, and departments. In the course of our pilgrimage and meetings, we visited the Vatican Secretariat of State, which is probably the oldest diplomatic mission in the world, and the Congregation for the Evangelization of Peoples. We also visited the Apostolic Palace and had a banquet in the midst of the priceless art of the Vatican Museum. A highlight of the trip was celebrating Mass in the Chapel of St. John Paul II in St. Peter's, where his body rests within the altar.

Our group from the United States was scheduled to meet

with Pope Benedict XVI on March 4. A couple of weeks earlier, however, he had announced that he was resigning from his office as pope on February 28, so we were at his last general audience in the plaza, and we were the last group allowed to enter the Sistine Chapel before it was sealed for the conclave. Pope Benedict's last audience truly represented the nations of the world. Some pilgrims carried their national flags, some of which I did not even recognize. The pope's helicopter flew right over us as he left the Vatican to go to the papal retreat at Castel Gondolfo, as he did not want to be a distraction for the upcoming conclave.

It was quite an interesting time with cardinals arriving from around the world to Rome. The cardinals represent many places on earth and have the great responsibility of electing a new pope when the office is vacant, either by death or resignation. I had the opportunity to meet three cardinals, one from the United States, one from Bolivia, and one from Italy.

I noticed the following Latin inscription on one of the buildings of the offices of the Propagation of the Faith in Rome: *Euntes Docete Omnes Gentes,* which means "Go and Teach all Nations." The Church has this responsibility *ad gentes,* to the people of the world. This passage is from the commission of our Lord to His Apostles to teach, baptize, and to make disciples (see Mt. 28:19–20).

The Church is the Mystical Body of Christ and a family of Faith. Although there are many cultures and languages, we are brothers and sisters by virtue of Baptism. We profess every week in the Creed that we believe in One, Holy, Catholic, and Apostolic Church.

For this, I am extremely grateful.

At Pope Benedict's last public audience in 2013

With brother Eric on the roof of St. Peter's in 1996

CHAPTER 16

Medical Mission

*Is anyone among you sick? He should summon
the presbyters of the church, and they should pray
over him and anoint him with oil in the name of
the Lord, and the prayer of faith will save the sick
person, and the Lord will raise him up. If he has
committed any sins, he will be forgiven.*

—JAMES 5:14–15

In 2002, I was invited to participate in a week-long medical mission in the Dominican Republic by a doctor whom I knew from my first parish assignment. He had been on other medical missions, and I had recently served with him on a Cursillo team. I was asked to serve as a chaplain and a translator. There were others from my first parish assignment, and we joined with a group from Florida. At the time, I wasn't really sure what we would be doing, but, based mostly on Dr. Nick's enthusiasm, I welcomed the opportunity. We made our way from the capital, Santo Domingo, to the mountain village of Guayubal. We set up a temporary clinic in an old disco with tables, chairs, an examination room and a portable generator. The people in the area were humble and joyful. A permanent deacon and I stayed in the home of a local schoolteacher. I was impressed that the teachers were highly respected and considered local leaders. We saw about 400 patients in our makeshift clinic and even visited a couple of neighboring villages, and I baptized one infant girl who was very ill. We met in the evenings in the parish church and had great comradery and unity during the week. On the last day, as we were loading the trucks with all of our equipment, I was able to visit and sing with some local school children. Several of us looked forward to our return to Santo Domingo for the night and our return to the United States the next day.

As we were preparing to leave, Sr. Bernadette, the coordinator of the mission, said, "There is a woman who was too ill to come to the clinic. Can you go to visit her? She lives close to here, and this child will take you to her home."

I went with two doctors and one of our volunteers. The young boy brought us to a small home, and we met Francisca who was lying in a bed in the front room. She was very thin and certainly not well. These two excellent doctors took one look at her left foot, which was half-black with gangrene. They quickly concluded that there was nothing that they could offer: no medication, no surgery, and no referral. The town did not have a hospital, but they knew that, even if there was an available operating room, she was not strong enough to survive a foot amputation. Her remaining time on earth was judged to be short.

I knew that there was something very important that I could do, and this might have been the reason why Divine Providence brought me to that place. In the Person of Christ, I could offer the Sacrament of the Anointing of the Sick, which is a gift of grace and a prayer of healing of body and soul. I was there to absolve her of her sins in the name and person of our Savior. I could give her what the most gifted surgeon in the world could not. All was not lost with Francisca that day. The grace of the sacrament would help her in her suffering, and the God of mercy would call her to Himself.

I appreciate the fact that we are a team (*un equipo* in Spanish), and we all have our place. I truly appreciate the doctors, nurses, and volunteers who serve with compassion and proficiency. I am still inspired by the dedication that I saw in our group that week. The Pastoral Care of the Sick is at the core of the priesthood. After I had administered the Sacrament of the Anointing of the Sick, I imparted the Apostolic Pardon, which is a plenary indulgence that grants complete pardon of the temporal punishment of sins already forgiven. The rite for the Pastoral Care of the Sick entrusts priests to give the Apostolic Pardon to those whose physical condition is grave and who have no known unconfessed mortal sins, and its words bring spiritual peace to the ill person. The priest says, "By the authority which the Apostolic See has given me, I grant you a full pardon and the remission of all your sins in the name of the Father, and of the Son, + and of the Holy Spirit. Amen." I never saw Francisca before that day or after, but I was thankful that I had the opportunity to serve her spiritually as a priest.

We are instruments of God's mercy and peace.

CHAPTER 17

My Journey in Hispanic Ministry

*To the weak I became weak, to win over the weak. I
have become all things to all, to save
at least some. All this I do for the sake of the gospel,
so that I too may have a share in it.*
—1 COR. 9:22-23

Sometimes, I am asked how I came to speak Spanish, which, in truth, I am still learning. I smile as I reflect on this journey that actually dates back more than forty years. In high school, I was told that I needed to take a foreign language to be accepted into college. I was a little worried as I didn't really make good grades in English, and I didn't know what to take. Some of my classmates had taken Latin and had received poor grades, so I decided against that one. I settled on Spanish, which I took for two years. In those days, the emphasis was not on conversational Spanish, but it was a basic introduction to the language. I certainly never imagined in the seventies that Spanish would become my second language and that I would use it just about every day as a priest.

There are a few experiences that helped shape my outlook during my formation to the priesthood. On a mission trip to the Deep South with Glenmary, I was with a priest and a small group for a Mass in a barn for some migrant workers in rural Arkansas. Thirty Hispanic men lived in the barn in very humble conditions and worked on the farms of that area. That was my first experience with migrants. We also visited some Hispanics who worked on a Walking Horse breeding ranch in Tennessee and still some others on a trip to Texas, where I made my first tortilla in a pastoral visit to some parishioners.

As a seminarian, I recall going to a hospital in Charlotte to bring Communion to a parishioner following her surgery. As I was making my way through the hallway, a woman asked me, "Are you a priest?" I replied that I was not, but that I was a seminarian. She asked me if I would visit her father who was a patient and bring him Holy Communion, and I agreed.

When we entered the room, she said in perfect English, "We are from Bolivia, and he only speaks Spanish." We had a Communion Service, and she translated what I said into Spanish. I thought to myself, *I should learn how to communicate in Spanish for my future priestly ministry.*

Another time, I was in the North Carolina mountains heading to the parish in Spruce Pine. I had just stopped for gas on a rural stretch and I saw six Hispanic men standing alongside the road, apparently waiting for a ride. In that area, many Hispanics work for Christmas tree growers. I thought to myself, "This is a rural area. I would like to go over and speak to those men, but I don't speak Spanish."

In the seminary, I made a decision to learn Spanish. I took two classes in general Spanish and then two in pastoral Spanish. After my ordination in 1995, I thought that I would have a year or two to work my way into Hispanic Ministry. My first pastor, Fr. Walsh, told me upon my arrival at Holy Family in Clemmons, "Well, Mark, you have the responsibility for the pastoral ministry here, and you are also the chaplain to our Youth Group and to the Hispanic Community of Cristo Rey in Yadkinville. So I didn't have a year or two to work into it, but I had to jump right in. The families at Cristo Rey were very kind and patient with me. As the Mass was at noon, the Franciscan sister who was the director of the mission made a signup sheet for families to have me over for lunch after the Mass. Those were some great experiences.

After a few months, I recognized my limitations in communication in Spanish, especially with confessions, homilies, and pastoral counsel. I asked Bishop Curlin to allow me to participate in a language school in Mexico for about a month. He eventually responded, "If your pastor approves of it, then I approve it."

That Spanish immersion was a great experience for me. I lived with a family in Cuernavaca, Mexico, attended classes, and helped in a local parish. I also visited cathedrals, convents, shrines, and historical sites. The immersion opened my ears to the language and helped me to understand and communicate better. Over the past twenty-six years, I have been involved in Hispanic ministry in each of my parish assignments. After Clemmons, I served in Winston-Salem, Biscoe, Jefferson, Sparta, Charlotte, and now in Mooresville. Over the years, I have celebrated more than 1,500 Masses in Spanish and have probably baptized around 2,000 persons (mostly little children) in Spanish. There have also been many celebrations of Our Lady of Guadalupe, house blessings, quinceañeras, weddings, funerals, and family fiestas. My trips to Latin America and the pastoral ministry here in the diocese have greatly enriched my life and ministry.

As a pastor and seminarian supervisor, I have always encouraged our parochial vicars and seminarians to spend some time learning the Spanish language and the rich culture. I have also tried to explain over the years to parishioners why the diocese thinks that it is important to have Masses and pastoral ministry in Spanish. I remain convinced that it is well worth the effort. Participation at events such as the Eucharistic Congress demonstrate the tremendous energy and faith of the many Hispanics in our midst.

For me, this journey has been a joyful one.

At a parish celebration of
Our Lady of Guadalupe

CHAPTER 18

Mother's Day Reflections

*Honor your father and your mother, that you may
have a long life in the land which the LORD, your
God, is giving you.*
—EXODUS 20:12

O n Mother's Day, we remember and honor our mothers,
those living and those who have passed from this life.
I have many memories of my own mother and grandmothers and of the mothers whom I've known and seen in my
ministry.

As I celebrate the Holy Mass, especially on Sundays, I see
the beautiful sight of many mothers holding small children.
The image of a mother and child reminds me of the many ar-
tistic images of the Blessed Mother holding her Son and our
Lord. Children are at peace in the arms of their mothers, who
exemplify love, and grandmothers are usually beaming when
they are caring for their grandchildren (or presenting their
photos.) In my first year of ministry preparation in the small
town of Hartford, Kentucky, I met a woman in a nursing home
who was 107 years old. The year was 1988, so she would have
been born around 1881. Her age alone was impressive, and,
to this day, she was the oldest person that I have ever met.
Then she told me that she was a great-great-great grandmother!
That took me a while to comprehend. My grandmothers were
great-grandmothers at the time, and one of my grandmothers
died just a couple of years before becoming a great-great grandmother. I thought about all those generations in this woman's
family. Growing up in rural Kentucky, I imagined that she had

probably been a young bride and was probably a mother before she was twenty, a grandmother before she was forty, and then perhaps a great-grandmother by the time she was in her early sixties, which that still left about forty-five years for the next two generations.

In my time as a priest, I have celebrated the funeral Masses for both of my grandmothers and my mother. This was certainly not something that I thought of while I was in the seminary. On Mother's Day, I remember my father's mother, Louise Albanese Lawlor, who was born in Brooklyn. The family story was that they lived for a time in the shadow of Ebbetts Field. Both of her parents had been born in Italy, and she fit the description of the tough Italian American New Yorker. She worked for thirty-five years for the phone company and was proud of the fact that she started out as an operator with plug-in phone cables and worked her way up to supervisor. She was a true company woman. I remember hearing her say, "Wasn't it terrible when they broke up MA-BELL?"

I also fondly remember my mother's mother, Mary Magdalene Cecil Test, who was a native of Washington, D.C. Her father, my great grandfather, was a fireman, and their home parish was St. Peter's, which is near the U.S. Capitol, where many Catholic members of Congress attend Mass on Holy Days. She was one of the most pious persons I have ever known. She once told me as we were going up the escalator at the Smithsonian Institute that it was a "five-Hail Mary escalator," meaning that she could pray five Hail Mary's as we ascended. Shortly after her death in 2002 at the age of ninety-six, I bought a chalice in Mexico with an engraved image of Our Lady of Guadalupe. I inscribed the base with the words, "In loving memory of my grandmother – Mary Magdalene Cecil Test," and I always pause on March 4 to remember her.

Her small, two-room apartment was a like a religious gift store with crosses, statues, and images of saints and angels. She even had a small bust of Pope St. John Paul II, which was the first one that I had ever seen. She was always close to her pastors and to the sisters who worked in the parishes, and she was truly my inspiration in the ways of faith. She was a daily communicant for most of her adult years, and she knew the confession schedule for many of the parishes in Washington. When I was young, she taught me the practice of making the Sign of the Cross while passing a Catholic Church. Once, we were in a bus in Washington, and she made the Sign of the Cross. I looked around and didn't see a church. She saw me looking and then mentioned that the parish of St. Anne's was a couple of blocks over! She brought me to the Shrine of the Immaculate Conception when I was in the second grade, and this began for me a life-long affiliation with that holy place. After her death, I went straight to the shrine where I celebrated a Mass for her eternal peace in one of the chapels. She continues to inspire me, and she is truly missed. Farewell, dear Gram.

Of course, I remember my own mother, Josephine Anne Test Lawlor, on Mother's Day. She was named Josephine after her maternal grandmother and Anne after St. Anne, the grandmother of our Lord and the mother of Mary. My mother's parents were praying and hoping for a child. In 1936, about three years after their marriage, they went on a pilgrimage to the great Basilica of St. Anne de Beaupré outside Quebec City in Canada. They went up the holy staircase on their knees in prayer, and my mother was born (an only child) two years later. My grandmother always gave credit for my mother's life to the intercession of St. Anne. At the time of my mother's birth, my grandmother intended to name her Anne after the good saint, until her forceful mother, Josephine Senge Cecil said, "You are going to name her Josephine after me, aren't you?" She was named Josephine Anne, which then became Jo Anne and, then, simply Jo.

I admit that I quarreled with my mother at times. Sometimes, we disagreed over such topics as politics, philosophy, and religion. She had a streak of rebellion at times, and, if I had that time back now, I would certainly try to be more patient with her.

My mother loved her five children in an unconditional way, and I really believe that she exemplified a "mother's love." Although she frustrated me at times, I never doubted her love and concern. She had a sharp wit and, at times, a sharp tongue.

I will never forget her passing from this life very quickly at the young age of fifty-nine in 1998. I truly believe that it was by the grace of God that I was with her.

I don't think that there is another relationship quite like that with one's mother.

With Mom in Clemmons in 1996,
just one and a half years before her death at the age of fifty-nine.

CHAPTER 19

Goodbye, Dear Mother . . .

Observe, my son, your father's command,
and do not reject your mother's teaching
—PROVERBS 6:20

I t was a morning that I will always remember. I was in my hometown of Salisbury, but I was running a little late and was in a hurry to get back to my parish assignment at Our Lady of the Americas in Biscoe, some fifty-five miles away. I had already concelebrated the morning Mass in my home parish, prayed the morning prayer, had breakfast with a couple of parishioners, and picked up a couple of items that I needed. There was just enough time to stop by my parent's house to say goodbye and pick up my overnight bag from the hermitage. It was the Friday after Ash Wednesday in 1998. It was my first Lent in Biscoe, and I actually had a lot to do. I had a pastoral visit to a homebound parishioner, and I had to prepare for the Lenten devotions, the Stations of the Cross in the afternoon, and the evening's *El Via Cruces*, the Spanish equivalent, but, first, I would have to find the booklets in the storage closet.

The previous day, I had debated about whether I should go home at all due to my busy schedule. In reflection, I know that I was inspired to go home. I arrived in the evening and had a nice visit with my parents. My mother was a little sad that her arthritis had greatly limited her activities. She had trouble walking any distance at all and had pain in many of her joints. She was only fifty-nine but had been in noticeably declining health for several months. We chatted a little, and then I left to dine with a friend. I did not suspect that I would not hear her voice again.

As I turned my car down our street for that short farewell the next morning, I was surprised to see a fire truck in front of the house. I first wondered if there was a problem with the new gas insert in the fireplace that had recently been installed. As I drove closer, I saw that there was an ambulance behind the fire truck. Then I saw Dad on the front porch and two EMT's running across the lawn toward the house with a stretcher. My mind raced. I knew that it was Mom. I looked in my front seat and was relieved to see my pastoral care kit with the Oil of the Sick, my stole, and the Pastoral Care of the Sick book, which has the Rite of Anointing. Sometimes, I moved this kit back and forth between vehicles. I stopped the car, grabbed the kit, and ran into the house.

In the living room, seven emergency personnel were desperately trying to resuscitate mom as she lay motionless in the middle of the floor. Dad stood off to the side and didn't say anything. Somehow, I moved to the area above her head and began administering the Sacrament of the Anointing of the Sick. It was like a blur. I prayed the priestly prayers, "Through this holy anointing, may the Lord in His love and mercy help you with the grace of the Holy Spirit," and "May the Lord who frees you from sin save you and raise you up." I continued with the Litany of the Saints and the Apostolic Pardon: "May almighty God, release you from all punishments in this life and in the life to come. May He open to you the gates of paradise and welcome you to everlasting joy. Amen."

I had taken CPR years earlier while working for the government. I knew there was a short window of time for resuscitation, and I knew that we were at that threshold or had already passed it. Finally, the lead EMT said, "We must go to the hospital."

Dad and I followed the ambulance to the hospital, which is very close to our home. They continued their efforts in the emergency room while we waited outside in the hall. They finally came out and told us that her brain was dead and there was nothing more that they could do. The lead doctor approached us and asked if they could stop all heroic measures.

Dad said, "Of course." My older brother arrived, and we had a quiet moment with Mom's body in the E.R. The reality then began to sink in. My mother, who had given birth to me, had passed from this life.

As one of her children, I was with her in her last moments. By Divine Providence, I was with her as a priest to assist her journey to the next life. It was another reminder to me of the awesome responsibility of this vocation. It is a mystery.

Farewell for now, dear mother.

May the souls of the faithful departed, through the mercy of God, rest in peace.

CHAPTER 20

Tribute to Bishop Curlin

*Like a shepherd he feeds his flock; in his arms he
gathers the lambs, Carrying them in his bosom,
leading the ewes with care.*
—ISAIAH 40:11

I was blessed to host Bishop William Curlin's sixtieth anniversary Mass during my time at the Parish of St. Vincent de Paul in 2017. I was also honored to be a pallbearer at his funeral just seven months later. In his sixty and a half years of ordained ministry, he served faithfully as a parish priest, vocation director, auxiliary bishop in Washington, and Bishop of the Diocese of Charlotte. He was still active in ministry, especially with retreats, parish missions, Confirmations, Penance services, Masses in parishes, and the Pastoral Care of the Sick and the Dying until the end of his life. Bishop Curlin was a regular visitor to St. Vincent de Paul during my pastorate there, and it was always beneficial to hear his words of wisdom on Christmas Eve and at other celebrations.

I actually heard of Bishop Curlin's appointment as the Bishop of the Diocese of Charlotte from a Baptist Navy chaplain. The chaplain was visiting my seminary, St. Meinrad in Indiana, and he had just arrived from Washington, D.C., where the appointment had been announced. In my years at St. Meinrad before the internet was available, we were usually not the first ones to learn of news from the outside world!

A couple of days after the appointment, I received a letter from my grandmother, a native of Washington, and she joyfully wrote of our great fortune in having Bishop William Curlin as our new bishop. She wrote that she "had followed the career of this holy priest for many years." My grandmother worked for the federal government in Washington, and she often went to the noon Mass/devotion at Old St. Mary's in Washington when Fr. Curlin was their pastor in the 1970's. I later learned that my Aunt Margaret and Uncle Earle had been involved in various projects at Old St. Mary's during Fr. Curlin's pastorate.

At one of my first meetings with Bishop Curlin, he asked me about my upcoming ordination to the diaconate. I related to him my hope to be ordained at my home parish, Sacred Heart in Salisbury. I was fully prepared to make my case to him since I had been an altar server in the parish and was confirmed there. I was also ready to report that the parish had totally supported me through my years of formation, and I thought it would also be good for vocations. Bishop Curlin did not give me the chance to make my case. He simply smiled and said, "Mark, that's a great idea." He then picked up his calendar and offered me three dates. With little to no discernment, I immediately picked the first date that he offered, October 8, 1994. At my ordination to the diaconate, Bishop Curlin spoke these words to me in his homily,

> *"Mark, through the grace of Holy Orders and a bond with our Lord Jesus Christ, you will preach words that you never wrote, give answers to things that you never read in a book or heard in a class; you will see doors opened that you thought were closed forever, and you will find the one who lives in the kingdom of your soul shining through your ministry."*

Bishop Curlin preached prophetic words that day, and I know that he was preaching from the heart with a background of much pastoral experience.

My grandmother decided not to attend my diaconate ordination, as she was going to save her energy for my priestly ordination eight months later. In her eighty-ninth year, she was overjoyed that she was invited to dinner at Bishop Curlin's residence the night before the ordination. She had a joyful reunion with the priest whom she had admired for so long. As my grandmother lay critically ill in a hospital in 2002 at the age of ninety-six, Bishop Curlin wrote to her, expressing his prayers for her and the hope of eternal life and the mercy of God. The nurses read the letter to her several times. At my last meeting with my grandmother, just a couple of days before she was called from this life, she said, "Bishop Curlin will go straight to Heaven."

Years later, Bishop Curlin was in critical condition in the hospital and several of us prayed the rosary at his bedside. He passed quietly from this life.

Bishop Curlin always lived the priesthood as Pope St. John Paul II expressed: "The priest does not live for himself, but for the Church and for the sanctification of the People of God."

Thank you, Bishop Curlin.

Bishop Curlin's Sixtieth Ordination
Anniversary, 2017

"Gram" Madge Test and Bishop
Curlin, the evening before my
ordination, 1995

CHAPTER 21

Mexico

When you turn back to him with all your heart,
and with all your soul do what is right before him,
Then he will turn to you, and will hide his face
from you no longer.
—TOBIT 13:6

I have been to Mexico eleven times, more than to any other foreign nation. The first time was just a few days after my ordination in 1995, and the last time was in 2016. Over the years, I have established friendships with many of our southern neighbors. I have also enjoyed visiting religious and historical sites in Mexico. I have been to Aztec and Mayan ruins as well as preserved colonial centers. I have celebrated and concelebrated Masses in cathedrals, basilicas, parishes, missions, convents, schools, and homes. Some of the churches that I have visited are truly spectacular expressions of the Faith. I have experienced great hospitality on my trips and have many great memories.

On one trip, I remember that I spent a morning at the cathedral of Mexico City, where I concelebrated the Mass. This great cathedral, which has many chapels and works of art, is one of the oldest in the Americas and a place of much historical significance. It was built on the site of the major pyramid of the former Aztec capital, Tenochtitlan, which was the place where thousands of human sacrifices had occurred during Aztec rule. This aspect of Aztec culture was one that the Spanish conquerors and their chaplains found very appalling. The Spanish won the bloody battle for the Aztec capital in 1521 after much hardship and death on both sides. Mexico City was then built on the ruins of Tenochtitlan, and the cathedral was constructed on the site of the pyramid. It is reported that even some of the stone blocks from the pyramid were used in the construction of the cathedral. What had once been the place of human sacrifice in a pagan ritual that glorified the sun is the now the place for the Holy Sacrifice of the Mass, where we worship the eternal Son of God.

Unfortunately, in the first ten years after the Spanish conquest, there were not many converts to Christianity among the natives of Mexico. It was then that Our Lady appeared to an Aztec Christian, St. Juan Diego Cuauhtlatoatzin, in 1531 and requested that a shrine be built on the site. She then requested that he relay her message to the bishop. When the bishop requested some sign of Mary's request, our Lady provided the roses of December, which Juan Diego carried in his tilma. When he presented the roses to the bishop, the miraculous image was formed on his tilma, which, after 490 years, may still be seen in the Basilica of Our Lady of Guadalupe. The initial news of the apparitions and the miraculous image were a catalyst to increased Christian devotion and conversions, and historians estimate that in the first seven years after the apparitions, eight million native Mexicans accepted the Faith and were baptized. Today, copies of the image can be found throughout Mexico, the United States, and in many other countries. In Mexico, for example, it is not unusual to see the image in chapels, on buildings, in homes, in tattoos, on taxis, and on public buses.

The Shrine of Our Lady of Guadalupe is one of the Church's great pilgrimage sites, receiving some twenty million pilgrims annually, and, by some accounts, it is the principal Marian Shrine in the world. I have visited the basilica, which is not far from the cathedral, many times, where I have celebrated Mass, prayed the Rosary, and celebrated the Sacrament of Penance, both as a confessor and a penitent. Among the highlights of my trips to Mexico was the time that I was privileged to celebrate Mass in the small chapel of Tepeyac, which was built on the site of the apparitions and roses on the top of the hill.

In 1970, Pope St. Paul VI reaffirmed that Mary, under the

title of Our Lady of Guadalupe, is a Patroness of All the Americas, and, in recent years, Our Lady of Guadalupe has been invoked as a Patroness of the Unborn. Pope St. John Paul II canonized St. Juan Diego in the summer of 2002.

On my last trip to Mexico, I went primarily to concelebrate the fiftieth ordination anniversary Mass of my good friend, Bishop Jaime Rodriguez Salazar in the Basilica of Our Lady of Guadalupe. He recently retired from the office of bishop in Huánuco, Peru, and is now living in his native Mexico. He was truly a pastoral bishop in the highlands of Peru, and he visited the Diocese of Charlotte twice.

I hope to have the opportunity to visit Mexico again.

grounds and journeys, there was the common thread of a "calling" that brought us together.

Seminarians give us hope for the future priestly ministry of the Church, especially here in the Diocese of Charlotte. I pray for our seminarians, that they may persevere in their vocation. Over the years, I have written letters of recommendation for applicants to our seminarian program. A couple of these have been ordained to the priesthood, including Padre Gabriel Carvajal, who was born in Mexico. As a layman, Gabriel had been a big help to me during my time as the administrator of Our Lady of the Americas Church in Biscoe, especially with liturgical music and catechesis. He is now a pastor in the diocese.

I also recommended Fr. Fred Werth for our seminarian program. Fred was a parishioner and catechist of our mission in Sparta and had practiced law in Galax, Virginia, for about twenty-five years. His wife and daughter died in a terrible automobile accident caused by an impaired driver. Fred, who was driving, miraculously survived the tragic wreck. During his recovery, he demonstrated a strong faith through that storm and heard the voice of God calling him to a new life in Holy Orders. He was ordained at about the age of sixty. He is now a pastor in the diocese and is one of our "grandfather priests."

Regarding vocations, I believe that the call of the Lord Jesus still resounds today. To His first Apostles, Jesus simply invited them to follow Him. Families, of course, are called to provide a spiritual home and to support a child discerning the call of the Lord. Parents can't give the call, but their attitude will help one who is discerning. I think that my call was an invitation, not an order.

I don't really know why the Lord called me, but I am certainly blessed in this vocation.

CHAPTER 24

The Role of the Laity

Do you not know that a little yeast leavens all the dough? Clear out the old yeast, so that you may become a fresh batch of dough, inasmuch as you are unleavened. For our paschal lamb, Christ, has been sacrificed. Therefore let us celebrate the feast, not with the old yeast, the yeast of malice and wicked-ness, but with the unleavened bread of sincerity and truth.

—1 COR. 5:6-8

I believe that the above Scriptural passage may be applied to the laity of the Church. The yeast causes the dough to rise. It is a catalyst for change and for growth. This image especially applies to the laity, who are involved in all aspects of society. Consider such fields as business, law, finance, medicine, politics, economics, heath care, athletics, education, and public service. There are members of the faithful in all of these fields, very often in leadership positions. The Church calls them to live in accord with Christian ethics and to have a positive influ-ence on their environment.

The overall statistics for the Catholic Church are astound-ing. There are now more than one billion members of the Catholic Church, and there are many millions of baptisms ev-ery year throughout the world. Of the more than one billion Catholics, there are approximately 400,000 priests and about 800,000 religious sisters. The laity, therefore, account for about 99.999% of the Universal Church.

It is true that a faithful priest, bishop, or religious may

make a positive difference in our society. It is also true that members of the laity have contacts and opportunities in their respective fields that the clergy and religious do not have. For example, priests are not permitted to hold a publicly elected office. The members of the laity working within the realm of politics are called to promote legislation and policies that are consistent with our Faith and for the common good. I am not recommending that the members of the laity preach to their coworkers in their professional positions (although we all share in the mission of the Apostles). I am, however, stressing that one does not leave one's Faith at the door when one goes to work. One's priorities on the job should be consistent with the tenets of our Faith. If there is ever a conflict between one's Faith and the requirements of one's job, then one should pray about it. Perhaps, one can work through the normal channels to find some resolution. If not, one may pray about finding another job. A mechanic friend of mine once told me that he had been told by his supervisor to lie to customers regarding the repair work that had been done on their cars. He told me that to maintain his integrity he could no longer work for that company. There are many possible scenarios when it comes to issues like this. The laity have an apostolate in the world. As a member of the clergy, I appreciate their assistance in pastoral ministry and in their witness in the community.

The Code of Canon Law, which governs the overall struc- ture of the Church, lists various rights and obligations of the lay faithful. For example, the lay faithful have the right to free- dom in the choice of their state of life, and they have a right to a Christian education and ongoing formation in the Faith. The laity have the obligation by virtue of Baptism and Con- firmation to work for the spread and acceptance of the divine message of salvation among people everywhere. They are also bound to bring an evangelical spirit to bear on the order of temporal things and to give a Christian witness in carrying out their secular pursuits.

The laity may be likened to the yeast that promotes growth and a positive change. Let us strive to live as we believe.

CHAPTER 25

Angels, Our Heavenly Friends

Then he prayed, "Blessed be God,
blessed be his great name, and blessed be
all his holy angels."
—TOBIT 11:14

On September 29, the Church celebrates the Feast of the Michael, Gabriel, and Raphael, Archangels, and, on October 2, the Church celebrates the Feast of the Holy Guardian Angels. Every year, especially on these feasts, I reflect on the role of the angels.

The word angel comes to us from a Greek translation of the Hebrew word meaning "messenger." The angels are spiritual beings who have been created by God. They are of God's court and in God's service, and they serve as messengers to humans. Their role is to do the will of God. Traditionally, the Church teaches that the angels are intelligent, have swiftness of movement, and communicate among themselves. It is also believed, based on certain passages of Scripture, that there are a great number of angels who are organized in different orders or choirs.

Sts. Gabriel and Michael are well known because of their prominent place in the Bible. St. Gabriel visited Zechariah, the father of John the Baptist, in the Temple to relay the message of the birth of his son. He also visited the young Mary to announce that she would be the mother of the Savior (see Lk 1). Angels were also present at the Lord's birth singing, "Glory to God in the highest and on earth peace to those on whom his favor rests" (Lk 2:14). St. Michael is remembered in Scripture as a defender of Heaven and as captain of the heavenly host. In the Book of Revelation, it is related that a war broke out in Heaven. St. Michael and his angels battled the dragon and his angels. The rebellious angels were defeated and expelled from Heaven and thrown down to the earth (see Rev 12:7–9).

The angelic representation and unseen companion of every person on earth is known as a guardian angel. This is a traditional teaching of the Church, although it has not been defined as an article of Faith. The teaching is based on the following verse of our Lord: "See that you do not despise one of these little ones; for I tell you that in Heaven their angels always behold the face of my Father who is in Heaven" (Mt 18:10).

Traditionally, the guardian angel represents the person before God, watches over the person, defends him or her, helps with prayer and thoughts, and presents the soul of a just person to God after death. Because of their important role, it is clear that we should be grateful to our guardian angels, and there have been a number of times in my life when I have felt the presence of my guardian angel.

Almost fifty years ago, I was playing with some friends in the neighborhood and became upset about something that happened in the game, so I decided that I was going to leave. In my frustration, I blindly rode my bicycle straight down the driveway and directly into the path of a fast-moving car. The young driver slammed on her brakes instantly, and the car stopped just as it bumped me and pushed me over. Fortunately, I was not hurt, but, if the car had traveled just a few more feet, I would have been run over. Even now, I can still hear the echo of the screeching tires and brakes and the crying of the driver and her baby after the car stopped. For some reason, my life was preserved. There have been many times while driving that my guardian angel has helped me in spite of own poor judgment or tiredness. I remember once feeling a tap on my shoulder as I was about to fall asleep at the wheel on an interstate. It was as if my guardian angel was telling me, "You'll drive a little bit better with both eyes open."

Thanks, angels.

CHAPTER 26

Retreat for Priests

*He said to them, "Come away by yourselves to a
deserted place and rest a while."*
—MARK 6:31

E very year, our diocesan priest's retreat is scheduled during
the first week of October. The Diocese of Charlotte is
fortunate to have the Living Waters Reflection Center in
beautiful Maggie Valley, which was a gift of the late Fr. Michael
William Murphy. Fr. Murphy was ordained to the priesthood
at the age of eighty. At an age when most people are retired, Fr.
Murphy was just beginning his ministry as a priest.

A retreat is ideally a time of prayer, spiritual renewal, and
rest. All priests and religious are expected to participate in at
least one retreat each year, and there are mandatory retreats pri-
or to ordination or solemn vows. The Feast of St. Francis of
Assisi on October 4 typically falls within the days of our retreat,
and it gives us the opportunity to reflect on that humble man of
peace and harmony. After the Apostles and the Blessed Mother,
St. Francis is perhaps one of the most well-known saints in the
history of the Church.

I think the following passage from the Gospel of Mark helps
us to understand the purpose of a retreat: "The apostles gathered
together with Jesus and reported all they had done and taught.
He said to them, 'Come away by yourselves to a deserted place
and rest a while'" (Mk 6: 31). The Apostles had just returned
from their mission of preaching repentance, driving out demons,
and anointing and healing the sick (see Mk 6:7–13). The Apostles surely had much to think about and wanted to relate their

experiences with the Lord, so Jesus invited them to a "retreat."

I think that many of our parishioners realize that most priests serving in the diocese are busy. The parishes of the diocese are very active and growing, and priests have many pastoral and administrative responsibilities, and I know that I am fortunate to have these five days of prayer and fellowship with my brother priests and our bishop. It is really the only time that priests serving in the different regions of the diocese are able to spend much time together. In addition to a couple of nice hikes or bicycle rides, it is an opportunity to reflect on our calling and to look ahead with hope to new challenges in ministry. Every year, the diocese invites a priest or bishop to lead the retreat by providing morning and evening conferences. Often, our retreat leader is a scholar who has completed advanced studies or written books. I recall that one retreat director referred to the Pope St. John Paul II's 1992 Apostolic Exhortation *Pastores Dabo Vobis* ("I will give you pastors"). In that document, the late Holy Father wrote this about the ministry of priests:

> *In the Church and on behalf of the Church, priests are a sacramental representation of Jesus Christ—the head and shepherd—authoritatively proclaiming his word, repeating his acts of forgiveness and his offer of salvation—particularly in baptism, penance and the Eucharist, showing his loving concern to the point of a total gift of self for the flock, which they gather into unity and lead to the Father through Christ and in the Spirit. In a word, priests exist and act in order to proclaim the Gospel to the world and to build up the Church in the name and person of Christ the head and shepherd.*

> *This is the ordinary and proper way in which ordained ministers share in the one priesthood of Christ. By the sacramental anointing of holy orders, the Holy Spirit configures them in a new and special way to Jesus Christ the head and shepherd; he forms and strengthens them with his pastoral charity; and he gives them an*

*authoritative role in the Church as servants of the
proclamation of the Gospel to every people and of the
fullness of Christian life of all the baptized." (no.15)*

Someone may ask, "What is the purpose of a retreat?" It is
a time to step back and consider God's blessing and our call to
follow the Lord. It may be compared to having one's batteries
recharged and having the instrumentation recalibrated. We all
need time for reflection and quiet prayer, and I'm convinced
that all people of faith will benefit from a retreat. It will help
us over the long journey.

Jesus said, "Come away by yourselves to a deserted place
and rest a while," and I encourage all of the Faithful to take a
break and to participate in a retreat if they have the opportunity. At a minimum, try to spend at least some time in quiet
prayer before the Blessed Sacrament.

And please remember to pray for priests and for those discerning a vocation in the Church.

CHAPTER 27

The Faith of our Fathers

As a father has compassion on his children,
so the LORD has compassion on those who fear him.
—PSALM 103:13

T he third Sunday of June is a time to remember and honor our fathers, those living and those who have been called from this life. This celebration was first promoted in the United States more than one hundred years ago. While such cultural holidays are not equivalent to the Solemnities of the Church, they nonetheless provide us with the opportunity to pause, to pray for, and to remember our fathers. Remember the commandment: "Honor your father and your mother, that you may have a long life in the land which the LORD, your God, is giving you" (Ex 20:12).

I must admit that I was taken aback the first time that a parishioner said, "Happy Father's Day," shortly after my ordination twenty-six years ago. I was also surprised a few years ago when a parishioner placed a very nice Smith and Wesson lock-blade knife in the collection basket with a note that said, "Happy Father's Day, Fr. Mark." Since the early Church, people have addressed their priests and spiritual leaders with the title of "Father." St. Paul even referred to himself as a father in his first letter to the Corinthians.

I know that I was blessed to have my father, Michael, and I appreciate all the sacrifices that he made for the family. I remember him helping me move from Raleigh to Charleston after I graduated from college. He also helped me move from Biscoe to the parish in Jefferson after I was named pastor there.

I often hear of fathers in our parish helping sons and daughters to move, which is a great work of mercy! There was an interesting connection between my father and myself. When dad was a young engineer at the time of my birth, he worked in the Philadelphia Naval Yard helping to build an aircraft carrier, the USS Kitty Hawk. After college, as a young engineer, I went to work in the Charleston Naval Shipyard helping to repair nuclear submarines.

Both of my grandfathers died prior to my birth. My father's father, George Michael Lawlor, whose parents were from Ireland, was born in Manhattan. He was an electrician and worked in construction. He even worked on one of the tunnels connecting Manhattan to the mainland. He was also very handy at fixing things. He died just two months before my birth in 1961.

Years ago, I was at a mission meeting in midtown Manhattan, and I looked up the address where he was born. It was actually very close to where I was staying, so I walked to the address and saw a high-rise building on the site. When he was born, there were row-houses there in what was then the Irish section of town. I noticed on his birth certificate that his home number was 15302, but that he was born at 15304. I was curious about this, and so I asked dad about it. He said that his father was the fourth or fifth child born, so his mother went next door to have her baby. I smiled and thought, *That is certainly a nice neighbor to say, "I know that it is a little hectic in your home with all your children. You can come over here to have your new baby!"*

My mother's father, William Hart Test of Washington, D.C., died at the young age of fifty. It was very hard for my mother who was an only child. She was only sixteen when he died of a heart attack on the living room sofa. He was a talented commercial artist, a band leader (a former member of the Marine Corps Band), and a magician. My mother played the cello with him and was his assistant in magic shows. He was originally an American Baptist but became Catholic just before he married my grandmother.

I do remember my great-grandfather, Giovanni Albanese,

who was born in Bari, Italy.

At the age of twenty-nine years old, he left from the port of Naples on the Prinz Adalbert (which was sunk in World War I) and arrived in New York City on October 25, 1905, in search of a better life, and he arrived ready to work. The ship's records note that he was single, that he did not speak English, and that he had about four dollars with him. Within a few years, he married Teresa Matrapasqua, also of Italy, and, over the years, they raised six children. My grandmother and godfather were two of these. Years later, "John," Teresa, and the family moved from Brooklyn to Bayside, Queens, which was considered a move to the "country" in those days, where my great-grandfather eventually started a couple of businesses—first a vegetable store and then a car battery store. Everyone called him "Pop." He was already pretty old when I was born, but he was very active until his death at the age of one hundred. He was even betting on horse races in his later years!

From working class beginnings, all the children did very well. I have been told that my great-grandfather was very proud to present four stars in the front window of their home during World War II, signifying that four family members were serving in the armed forces. At the time that he was celebrating his hundredth birthday in 1976, the nation was celebrating the bicentennial, and he received a congratulatory letter from President Jimmy Carter.

My maternal grandmother gave me a photo of one of my great-great-great grandfathers, Julius Frederick Veidt, who was born in Brunswick, Germany, in 1822. He came to the United States in 1848 and served in the U.S. Army during the Civil War. One of my relatives wrote an account of his life, and I found it amazing to learn how many of his descendants are now living. I have many relatives just through this part of our family, although I don't know them, and one of my relatives told me that we have other distant cousins in Hamburg, Germany.

When we think of or honor our fathers, we should also remember God our loving Father, the first Person of the Blessed Trinity. The *Catechism of the Catholic Church* teaches that God the Father transcends the categories of the created world. We may invoke God as "Father" because He is revealed to us by His Son who became a man and because His Spirit makes Him known to us (see *CCC* 2779–2780). Jesus has shown humanity the way to the Father. He said, "I am the way and the truth and the life. No one comes to the Father except through me" (Jn 14:6). Jesus taught us of the Father's mercy and compassion in the Parable of the Prodigal Son, which is really the "parable of the compassionate father" (see Lk 15). The father waited for his son to return and restored him to his place in the family. Scripture has it that "God is love, and whoever remains in love remains in God and God in him" (1 Jn 4:16).

In reflecting on God the Father, we have reason to be hopeful. God is just, and yet God is merciful.

CHAPTER 28

The Screen Porch Door: Dad's Passing

*Seventy is the sum of our years, or eighty, if we are
strong; Most of them are toil and sorrow; they pass
quickly, and we are gone.*
—PSALM 90:10

For many years, on Monday mornings around 7:20 am,
I would hear the distinctive sound of the slamming of
the screen porch door from my neighbor's house. That
sound informed me that my father was on his way over for
our 7:30 am morning Mass and that he would arrive at my
back door in about thirty seconds. Like many priests, I look
forward to getting a break on my day off. On Sundays, after
the last Mass, the last baptism, the last confession, or the last
meeting, I usually head to my cottage of refuge in my hometown of Salisbury. After my ordination, I used to concelebrate
the morning Mass on my day off in my home parish of Sacred
Heart. After my mother's death in 1998, my father, who had
already retired, began to attend as well. He mentioned to me
that as mom had been called quite suddenly from this life at
the age of fifty-nine, he recognized the reality that he could be
next, and so he desired to prepare. For years, a small group of
us would pray Morning Prayer after the Mass and then go out
for breakfast. After a while, one of my brothers, Eric, who was a
lector, also began to join us for the Monday Mass and breakfast.

Eventually, I bought Dad's back lot and built a modest
ranch home for my day off and possible future retirement. Dad
then sold the old home place and started his new phase of life
as a renter. Shortly thereafter, the little bungalow beside mine

became available, and I asked Dad if he would move there if I could get a loan to buy the house. He said that he always liked that little house and that he would like to live there. It was an interesting turn of events. I had rented from Dad for nine years, and now he rented from me! I promised him that I would never raise his rent and that he could live in the house for as long as he wanted. We eventually began to celebrate the Monday morning Mass in my house, and, afterwards, I would cook breakfast for Dad and my brother Eric. When we first started, I would ask Dad and Eric what they wanted for breakfast. After a while, I felt as though I was a short-order chef, and so I decided that I would select what we would have for breakfast. When I broke the news to them, Dad responded with great sarcasm, "Oh, so now it's like prison food. The prisoners don't get a choice either!" Over breakfast, we usually had a lively discussion over the latest political news, current events, and the intrigue in town and in the local parish. Dad would sometimes inform us of his latest health fad, investment strategy, or conspiracy theory. We called ourselves the three bachelors and enjoyed many Monday mornings together in my home over eleven years.

Dad, who was a fine engineer and a brilliant mathematician, was in many ways a humble man who didn't mind the cheap seats, bargain brands, or even cheap wine. In July of 2015 on a Monday morning, I was in my easy chair and, at 7:20, I didn't hear the slam of the screen porch door from next door. It was an eerie silence. At 7:30, Eric arrived and asked, "Where's Dad?" I told him that I didn't know as he was always punctual. When I had arrived from Charlotte on Sunday evening, I saw his light on and his car in the driveway. I usually didn't check in with him if it was already Sunday evening. We quickly went next door with some anxiety. Entering the home through the front door with my key, we found Dad lifeless on the floor, apparently from a massive heart attack. It was a sight that we will certainly never forget. Our father, our travel companion, and our friend had been called from us to his eternal home. Dad was eighty. As I was preparing the homily for his funeral Mass just three days later, a verse from Psalm 90 came to mind:

"Seventy is the sum of our years, or eighty, if we are strong" (v. 10). I thought to myself, *Dad would be pleased to know that he was considered strong by the psalmist.*

Eric and I continue the tradition of Monday morning Mass and breakfast. There is, however, an empty space around the dining room table that serves as the altar. Like many others, we miss our father.

Eternal peace be with you, Dad.

The three bachelors at a Castle Banquet in Ireland in 1999

CHAPTER 29

Maritime Ministry

God called the dry land "earth," and the basin of
water he called "sea."
God saw that it was good.
—GENESIS 1:10

While I was working as an engineer, I recall hearing a priest mention something in his homily relating his past experience of serving as a chaplain on a cruise ship. I thought that that sounded great! I heard a little more about it while I was in the seminary and decided that I would look into the possibility of it after I was ordained. Some years later, I received a brochure from the Apostleship of the Sea (AOS), which reaches out to mariners, fisherman, and all who work or travel the waterways of the world. It is a Catholic ministry that provides for the sacramental life of those at major ports or onboard ships. Each diocesan priest is required to have his bishop's permission to participate, and, at the time, there were several hundred priests in the United States who were members of the Apostleship of the Sea.

In 1920, Pope Pius XI bestowed his apostolic blessing on the ministry and encouraged its expansion. In most major countries, a bishop promoter oversees the work of a national director, who coordinates and assigns the chaplains. The ministry has become well known for serving on cruise ships, but other chaplains serve on merchant vessels, hospital ships, shore clinics, and in maritime academies.

In his Apostolic Letter on the Apostleship of the Sea (January 31, 1997), Pope St. John Paul II wrote:

The "Star of the Sea" has long been the favorite title by which mariners have called on her in whose protection they have always trusted: the Blessed Virgin Mary. Jesus Christ, her Son, accompanied the disciples in their boat, helped them in the labors and calmed the storms. Thus the Church also accompanies mariners, taking care of the specific spiritual needs of those who for various reasons live and work in the maritime world.

Maritime chaplains have been around for centuries. The first priests to arrive in the New World sailed with Christopher Columbus. Magellan also had priests with him on his epic voyage. St. Peter Claver was a holy priest who served as a chaplain in the port of Cartagena, Columbia. He cared for the ill and poor slaves who arrived in bondage. We recall, as well, the voyage of St. Paul to Rome by sea (see Acts 27–28).

I signed on for the first time to serve as the Catholic chaplain on a cruise ship. It was actually a very relaxing ten days. We visited five Caribbean islands on our voyage of some 3,200 nautical miles. It was great to have a short respite from the burdens and demands of parish administration and the phones! The duties of an AOS chaplain are to celebrate daily Masses for the passengers and another Mass on Sunday evening for the crew. The chaplain is also available for the Sacraments of Penance and the Anointing of the Sick and to offer pastoral care and counseling to those who request it. The priest's stipend for his ministry is a small cabin and his meals. Not bad! Before the cruise of 2005, I decided that I would try it once, and, if it worked out well, I would consider it again. Since it did go well, I served again on an Alaskan cruise on the Holland American Line from Seattle to Juneau and back. We visited the ports of Ketchikan, Sitka, and Victoria, British Columbia.

I fully acknowledge that those of us who have been called to the ordained priesthood have a wonderful life and great opportunities for ministry. There is certainly a lot to do at times, and a pastor has a great responsibility for the care of souls. And I am convinced that those of us who have been called to serve as priests will experience great fulfillment. However, I appreciate the opportunity for a yearly retreat, a day off, and vacations, all of which are supported in *The Code of Canon Law*.

The views from a ship, especially sunrises and sunsets, are like looking at God's masterpiece.

CHAPTER 30

Respecting Life

Then God said: Let us make human beings in our image, after our likeness. Let them have dominion over the fish of the sea, the birds of the air, the tame animals, all the wild animals, and all the creatures that crawl on the earth. God created mankind in his image; in the image of God he created them; male and female he created them.
—GENESIS 1:26-27

S ome years ago, at a book sale at a public library, I purchased a book titled *Atoms, Energy and Machines*. The
book was printed in 1957, and I believe that I paid fifty
cents for it. My interest in the book was that it provided some
of the basic principles, such as motion, structures, and physics,
that I had studied in much greater detail for my degree in mechanical engineering. I no longer have many of the texts that
I used in college, nor do I have much time for the study of
engineering.

There is an interesting chapter in this book that begins
with the question: What makes a man? The chapter looks at a
typical human body as a collection of elements. For example,
the text notes that there is enough fat in a typical body to make
seven bars of soap and enough iron to make a medium-sized
nail. There is also enough phosphorus to make 2,200 match
heads and enough sugar to sweeten a gallon of lemonade. In
the complete analysis, there are twenty elements in the human
body (not counting gold teeth or artificial limbs), and if they

were sold as raw materials, the body would be worth about one dollar. Allowing for inflation since 1957, the materials today might be worth about six dollars.

This scientific analysis of human value is quite different from the value given it by our Faith. We believe that human life has been created in the image and likeness of God. The one thing that is not noted in the scientific analysis of the human body is the existence of the soul, which survives physical death. Each human being has inestimable value. St. Paul wrote, "Do you not know that your body is a temple of the holy Spirit within you, whom you have from God, and that you are not your own? For you have been purchased at a price. Therefore, glorify God in your body" (1 Cor 6:19–20).

The body is a temple of the Holy Spirit, and we have been purchased at a price that is much more than a few dollars. We have been redeemed by the perfect sacrifice of Calvary. Our Lord died that we may have eternal life, and we believe in the sanctity of life.

The first Sunday of October has been designated as "Respect Life Sunday," and the theme continues throughout the month of October. In our prayers, we give thanks to God for our lives and for our families. As a people of faith, our belief that God is the author of life is central and foundational. The Catholic Church teaches that life should be respected and nurtured from conception to natural death. When asked about the greatest commandment of the Law, our Lord responded that: "You shall love the Lord, your God, with all your heart, with all your soul, and with all your mind. This is the greatest and the first commandment. The second is like it: You shall love your neighbor as yourself. The whole law and the prophets depend on these two commandments" (Mt 22:37–40). The love of God and the love of neighbor thus fulfill the law of God.

In 1995, Pope St. John Paul II published the encyclical *Evangelium Vitae* ("The Gospel of Life"). During his ministry as the Vicar of Christ, the pontiff consistently called the faithful and the people of the world to respect life. In this encyclical, he wrote:

The texts of Sacred Scripture . . . show such great respect for the human being in the mother's womb that they require as a logical consequence that God's commandment You shall not kill be extended to the unborn child as well. Human life is sacred and inviolable at every moment of existence, including the initial phase, which precedes birth. . . . . when they are still in their mother's womb, . . . they are the personal objects of God's loving and fatherly providence. (No. 61)

In hope, we peacefully pray, especially through the Holy Rosary, for the conversion of hearts of those who are opposed to God's precious gift of life. As prayerful witnesses, I have stood with faithful witnesses in the Life Chain. I have prayed at abortion clinics and admire those who strive to offer the women entering these dark chambers with "life alternatives." I have walked with faithful people in the annual March for Life in Washington, D.C., and in local marches.

Together, we can make a difference.

CHAPTER 31

Mission Pilgrimage along El Camino Real (the Royal Highway)

Go, therefore, and make disciples of all nations, baptizing them in the name of the Father, and of the Son, and of the holy Spirit, teaching them to observe all that I have commanded you. And behold, I am with you always, until the end of the age.
—MATTHEW 28:19-20

S ome years before I was ordained, during a visit to my grandmother in Washington, D.C., I went over to the U.S. Capitol and just roamed around. In those days, the doors were open, and I don't recall any security check. I recall seeing a statue of a man wearing Franciscan robes holding a church in one hand and a cross in the other. The base of the statue was engraved with the name "Serra."

At the time, I didn't know anything about the man the statue represented. I have since learned that it represents Padre Junípero Serra, a Franciscan priest from Spain who is considered the builder of the State of California. St. Junípero is one of four Catholic priests honored in the Statuary Hall in the U.S. Capitol. Ever since I saw that statue, I became interested in the missions of California.

In 2017, I decided to make a pilgrimage to the twenty-one original missions of California that were founded by the Franciscans from 1769 to 1823. It was originally planned as a group pilgrimage, but not enough pilgrims signed up. I then decided to make the trip on my own.

It was a spiritual journey, and I learned a lot of history

while being inspired by the missionary zeal of the Franciscans. Our Lord gave his Apostles the commission to: "Go, therefore, and make disciples of all nations" (Mt 28:19). With the colonization of the New World, missionaries sought to bring the joy of the Gospel to the natives living on this continent. Fr. Junípero Serra arrived in Mexico from Spain as a missionary. He was then sent to California where he established the first mission of San Diego. He would go on to establish eight more missions before his death in 1784.

At his beatification ceremony in 1988, Pope St. John Paul II said that Fr. Serra was "a shining example of Christian virtue and the missionary spirit." He learned the languages of seven different tribes and prepared a catechism for each. He also worked with the natives and helped them to develop farming techniques and the making of baskets, leather products (such as saddles), and other items that could be used in trade. The Franciscans planted the first grapes and oranges in California and also started the first school. There were times when the good padres stood between the natives and the Spanish soldiers who were in the area to protect the missions, but who did not always practice the Christian virtues.

The Franciscans did not believe in forced conversions but always sought to live in accord with Gospel values to teach the Faith. There were thousands of baptisms during the mission period. Today, there are some ten million Catholics in California, whose faith is rooted in these early missions, and the major cities of California had humble beginnings as Franciscan missions. For example, the mission of San Gabriel provided the seed for the modern City of Los Angeles, which is today the second largest city in the nation.

The missions began under the jurisdiction of Spain, but, after Mexico gained independence from the Spanish crown in 1721, they were under Mexican rule. The Franciscans were dismissed by the authorities of Mexico in 1834 in a time of secularization. During the war with Mexico in the 1840's, some of the missions were actually occupied by U.S. forces. Some missions fell into disrepair or suffered from earthquakes or fires. California became a U.S. state in 1850, and most of the missions were returned to the Catholic Church by American presidents, including Abraham Lincoln shortly before his assassination. Today, nineteen of the original missions are connected with or are serving as parishes, and two are part of the California State Park system. Several have Catholics schools connected with them, and the old Mission of Santa Clara is in the middle of the campus of Santa Clara University. The missions still serve the Church as this pilgrim can attest. At the Mission of San Raphael, for example, Mass is celebrated in five languages every Sunday: English, Spanish, Portuguese, Vietnamese, and Haitian!

These parishes inspired by the early missionaries are a reminder that our Faith is built on those who blazed the mission trail before us. At the canonization of Blessed Junípero during his pastoral visit to the United States in 2015, Pope Francis said the following:

> Father Junípero Serra was the embodiment of "a Church which goes forth." He was excited about blazing trails, going forth to meet many people, learning and valuing their particular customs and ways of life. He learned how to bring to birth and nurture God's life in the faces of everyone he met; he made them his brothers and sisters. Junípero sought to defend the dignity of the native community, to protect it from those who had mistreated and abused it. Father Serra had a motto which inspired his life and work, a saying he lived his life by: ¡siempre adelante! Keep moving forward! For him, this was the way to continue experiencing the joy of the Gospel, ... He kept moving forward, because the Lord was waiting. He kept going, because his brothers and sisters were waiting. He kept going forward to the end of his life. Today, like him, may we be able to say: Forward! Let's keep moving forward!

The Missionaries have blazed the trail before us!

CHAPTER 32

Faithful Service

*Yet these also were godly; their virtues
have not been forgotten.*
—SIRACH 44:10

I n the previous chapter, I noted that I had first learned about
St. Junípero Serra on a casual visit to the U.S. Capitol many
years ago. I later learned that it was by an Act of Congress
in 1864 that each state was asked to donate two statues of those
who played an important role in the history of their state for the
National Statuary Hall and other places in the Capitol. Among
those represented are thirteen Catholics, including four priests
and one nun. It is interesting to me that these five religious
were all born in different countries. The leaders of each state in
the union could have chosen any two people from their history
for this honor, so I think that it is worthy to recount a brief history of these four priests and the religious sister in this chapter.

I will begin with St. Junípero Serra, whom I wrote about
in the previous chapter. Padre Junípero Serra of Spain was a
Franciscan friar who founded nine of the missions in present
day California as well as a number of missions in Mexico. He
reportedly baptized some six thousand Native Americans and
is considered the builder of the State of California. His remains
are under the altar at the Mission in Carmel, which is a place
of pilgrimage and public veneration. Both Spain and the United States have honored St. Junípero Serra with his image on a
postage stamp.

Father Eusebio Francisco Kino, S.J., of Italy was a Catholic priest who became known as the "Padre on Horseback" in

what is now northwestern Mexico and the southwestern United States. He is remembered for his exploration of the region and for his ministry in the evangelization of the Native American population. He established twenty-four missions and was known for his ability to create relationships between indigenous peoples and the Church that he represented. Father Kino has been honored both in Mexico and the United States, and he represents Arizona in Statuary Hall.

Michigan donated the statue of Fr. Jacques Marquette, S.J., to the Capitol. He was a French Jesuit missionary who founded Michigan's first European settlement, Sault Ste. Marie and, later, St. Ignace, Michigan. He died after a bout of dysentery in 1675 at the young age of thirty-eight. He was also honored by the U.S. Postal Service with his image on a stamp.

St. Damien of Molokai, SS.CC., from Belgium volunteered to go to the Kingdom of Hawaii in 1864. After serving in various missions, he volunteered to serve on the Island of Molokai, which was a government-sanctioned quarantine for those afflicted with Hansen's disease (leprosy). After sixteen years of caring for the physical, spiritual, and emotional needs of those in the leper colony, Fr. Damien eventually contracted the disease, which took his life. He is considered a "martyr of charity."

The religious sister honored in statuary hall is Mother Mary Joseph Pariseau of the Sisters of Charity of Canada. She was a pioneer missionary and humanitarian. She founded the first hospital in the northwest in Washington State.

Also represented in the U.S. Capitol Statuary Hall are lay Catholics who served in government posts or in exploration. It is beneficial for us to know the history of this country and to recognize those of our Faith who have contributed to the Church and to the greater society. The United States is the home of some 77 million Catholics, which amount to about twenty-three percent of the overall population. Members of the Catholic Church serve in practically every aspect of society and are often leaders in their fields.

The Apostle Paul encouraged prayer for those in positions

of authority and encouraged the Church to "live as children of light, for light produces goodness and righteousness and truth" (Eph 5:8–9).

Our goal should be for building up society as we live our Faith.

CHAPTER 33

The Potential of Seeds

Hear this! A sower went out to sow.
—MARK 4:3

I n our hemisphere, Easter is celebrated in the spring, which is a time in nature for new life and growth. After the winter, it seems as though some plants and trees burst to life with the changing of seasons. In the spring, I look for the new growth on my fruit trees and plants. A couple of years ago, I was quite amazed to see perhaps 1,000 blooms on one of my peach trees and several hundred on a plum tree. I thought, *Perhaps, I can start Padre's Fruit Stand on weekends to help pay off our parish debt!*

In the summer, I hope to pick and enjoy fresh apples, peaches, pears, plums, cherries, blueberries, raspberries, strawberries, grapes, tomatoes, lemons, oranges, and key limes. The squirrels, the birds and even the ants also share in the abundance! All of these fruits have seeds that could be planted to increase the produce in the future. Jesus began the Parable of the Sower with the words, "A sower went out to sow " (Lk 8:5). In the parable, some of the seeds fell on the path, some fell on rocky ground, some fell among thorns, and some fell on good soil where it produced fruit a hundredfold. In the explanation of the parable, Jesus said, "The seed is the word of God" (Lk 8:11).

I think that the message of the parable is twofold for us. We are called to be the good soil that receives the Word and produces fruit for the Kingdom of God. We are also called into service to plant and nurture the seeds of faith and righteousness in the world. For a number of years, I have been very interested in the potential of seeds. About twenty years ago, I started a small garden, which was something that I had wanted to do for years. I recently planted some tomato seeds that I have had for a few years. The small plants are now growing. A seed will not grow until it is planted. By planting and nurturing, its potential will be realized.

As a spiritual reflection, we may ponder the question: What seeds am I planting? Am I planting seeds of peace and reconciliation, of patience and kindness, of charity and hope?

Scripture tells us that "a person will reap only what he sows . . . the one who sows for the spirit will reap eternal life from the spirit. Let us not grow tired of doing good, for in due time we shall reap our harvest, if we do not give up" (Gal 6:7–9).

The seed of faith was planted in our souls at the time of Baptism.

Let us continue to nurture the seed of faith.

CHAPTER 34

The Sacrament of Baptism

We were indeed buried with him through baptism
into death, so that, just as Christ was raised from
the dead by the glory of the Father, we too might live
in newness of life.
—ROMANS 6:4

The Feast of the Baptism of our Lord closes the liturgical season of Christmas. Of course, someone may wonder, "Why was our Lord baptized?" Jesus had no sins and, therefore, had no need to repent. He is the Divine Son of God and our Lord and Savior. One teacher of the early Church wrote that Christ was not baptized to be made holy by the water, but to make the water holy. He was baptized to show us the way and to consecrate the new sacrament. In His commissioning of the Apostles, Jesus told them, "Go, therefore, and make disciples of all nations, baptizing them in the name of the Father, and of the Son, and of the holy Spirit, teaching them to observe all that I have commanded you. And behold, I am with you always, until the end of the age" (Mt 28:19–20).

Baptism is the beginning of a life of grace. It is a spiritual rebirth and the first Sacrament of Initiation. There are two major benefits that we receive from Baptism. First, it washes away Original Sin. This is the sin that all have inherited through human generation since the first couple chose to disobey God. The second benefit of Baptism is that it incorporates us into the Family of God, the Church, which is the Mystical Body of Christ.

Baptism is also a joyful sacrament. I am able to say this

from a pastoral perspective. There is joy for the family, the parish, and for the Universal Church. Over the past twenty-six years, I have baptized at least 2,500 persons. On a mission trip to the jungle region of Peru, one pastor and I baptized about seventy children in one afternoon. I have always considered it a great honor to welcome new members into the family of faith through Baptism. In a sense, it is like I am opening the door of the Church for them to enter.

Baptism is also a sacrament that requires Christian responsibility. At the Baptism of an infant child, the parents accept the responsibility of raising the child in the Church and teaching the child the way of faith through word and example. At the Baptism of one who has reached the age of reason (about seven years old), the person accepts the responsibility of living in the light of the Faith and keeping his or her baptismal promises. The godparents as well accept the responsibility of assisting the parents of the child in their role as Christian parents. For adults, who are received into the Church at the Easter Vigil, the sponsors are to be spiritual companions.

Godparents are encouraged to remember and celebrate the baptismal anniversaries. I became very close to my godfather while I was in the seminary. Uncle Fred, a younger brother of a grandmother, was also my father's godfather. He died in 1999, and I was very pleased that he was present at my ordinations as a deacon in 1994 and as a priest in 1995. I sometimes remind the godparents at the time of a Baptism that it is unlikely that the child's birthday will ever pass without notice. It is important for them to celebrate the anniversary of their baptism, which is a spiritual rebirth.

The blessed water in the fonts by the doors of parish churches and chapels reminds us of the saving waters of baptism. When we bless ourselves with the Holy Water, we should be thankful for the grace of our own baptism. We should also make a petition for protection and for good health. The blessed water of baptism is also used for the blessing of articles such as rosaries, crucifixes, automobiles, and homes.

Every year, when we celebrate the Feast of the Baptism of

Jesus in the River Jordan, we should remember with joy the grace of our own baptism, even if we don't remember the actual celebration.

We thank God for the grace of faith, and we humbly ask for continued guidance to live in the light of the Gospel.

CHAPTER 35

Ill and You Cared for Me

When did we see you ill or in prison, and visit you?'
And the king will say to them in reply,
'Amen, I say to you, whatever you did for one of
these least brothers of mine, you did for me.'
—MATTHEW 25:39-40

Prayer, fasting, and almsgiving are emphasized during the Holy Season of Lent. These may be considered the pillars of a balanced Christian life, and almsgiving may be considered as giving from the heart. The corporal works of mercy are derived from our Lord's teaching on the final judgment from the Gospel of Matthew.

"When the Son of Man comes in his glory, and all the
angels with him, he will sit upon his glorious throne,
and all the nations will be assembled before him. And
he will separate them one from another, as a shepherd
separates the sheep from the goats. He will place the sheep
on his right and the goats on his left. Then the king will
say to those on his right, 'Come, you who are blessed by
my Father. Inherit the kingdom prepared for you from
the foundation of the world. For I was hungry and you
gave me food, I was thirsty and you gave me drink, a
stranger and you welcomed me, naked and you clothed
me, ill and you cared for me, in prison and you visited
me.' Then the righteous will answer him and say, 'Lord,
when did we see you hungry and feed you, or thirsty
and give you drink? When did we see you a stranger and

welcome you, or naked and clothe you? When did we see
you ill or in prison, and visit you?' And the king will say
to them in reply, 'Amen, I say to you, whatever you did
for one of these least brothers of mine, you did for me.'"
(Mt 25:31–40)

We are all called to see the face of the Lord among those
we help in our works of mercy. We do not earn Heaven by our
works. Rather, they are a response to God's grace—part of having
a "living faith." In the *General Introduction to the Sacrament of*
Anointing of the Sick, it reminds priests, and especially pastors,
that it is their sacred duty to care for the sick by personal visits
and other acts of kindness. In these visits, the priest brings the
sacraments of the Church, the Word of God, and the virtue of
hope. I have always sought to follow these instructions as a priest,
and visiting the sick is a regular part of my priestly ministry.

I certainly have a different perspective now than I had in
my youth. When I was in high school, my older brother worked
as a cleaning man in a nursing home. One evening, he needed a
ride home, and he asked me to pick him up from work. When
it was time to pick him up, he wasn't out front as I had hoped,
and I remember that I didn't even want to go in to find him. It
was like I did not want to see people who were incapacitated or
suffering. Perhaps, there was some sense of fear.

It would be more than ten years before I went back to another nursing home. At that time, I was on a service and vocation retreat in a small town in the hills of Kentucky. The retreat
included a trip to a nursing home to visit the residents and to
sing songs. We weren't exactly a big hit when we entered the
day room singing "When the Saint Go Marching In." One of
the dear residents actually shouted, "I don't want to hear that!
I want to go to bed!"

I remember that I still was not totally comfortable in that
environment, but I gradually came to see the importance of
pastoral care in ministry, especially to the elderly and those with
special needs. It is the will of the Lord that His healing ministry
continues in the Church, and, since my ordination in 1995,

the pastoral care to the sick and dying has been an integral component of my ministry, especially in hospitals, nursing care facilities, hospice units, and in family homes.

In his teaching on the Church as the one Body of Christ, St. Paul wrote: "If [one] part suffers, all the parts suffer with it" (1 Cor 12:26). For this reason, the Instruction to the Sacrament of Anointing of the Sick specifies "that all baptized Christians share in this ministry of mutual charity within the Body of Christ by doing all that they can to help the sick return to health, by showing love for the sick, and by celebrating the sacraments with them" (no. 34). It also encourages the family and friends to strengthen the sick with prayers and words of faith, commending them to the suffering and glorified Lord, and I greatly appreciate the witness of families and parishioners in their care of the sick.

It is important to remember that there are two Sacraments of Healing: The Sacrament of Penance and the Sacrament of Anointing of the Sick. The Lord Jesus is the Divine Physician of our bodies and souls. In the Sacrament of the Anointing, there is a conferral of grace and a prayer for the healing of body and soul. There are times when a spiritual healing may be much more profound than a physical healing.

Our illnesses or sufferings may be our sharing in the Cross of Christ:

> *"The special grace of the sacrament of the Anointing of the Sick has as its effects:*
>
> — *the uniting of the sick person to the passion of Christ for his or her own good and for that of the whole Church;*
>
> — *the strengthening, peace, and courage to endure in a Christian manner the sufferings of illness or old age;*
>
> — *the forgiveness of sins if the person is not able to obtain forgiveness through the Sacrament of Penance;*
>
> — *the restoration of health, if it is conducive to the salvation of his soul;*

> — *the preparation for the passing of this life to eternal life." (CCC 1532)*

We trust in His mercy and peace even in the midst of illness and suffering.

CHAPTER 36

St. Meinrad Archabbey and Seminary: The "Hill"

I rejoiced when they said to me, "Let us go to the
house of the LORD."
—PSALM 122:1

When I was candidate for the Glenmary Home Missioners, our formation house in Hartford, Kentucky, was only about an hour's drive from St. Meinrad Archabbey and Seminary in the southernmost county of Indiana. Although I never actually visited St. Meinrad in those days, I did drive by it once. It is like something out of Europe with the stone construction, the high tower, and the steeples all on a large hill. When I applied to the seminarian program for the Diocese of Charlotte, I knew that we had a couple of seminarians at St. Meinrad and also a couple studying in Washington, D.C., and Maryland. If I had been asked my preference, I would have expressed my desire to study in Washington, D.C. since my grandmother and some cousins lived in that area. I also knew my way around Washington, which is about 180 miles closer to my home than southern Indiana.

Well, I wasn't asked where I desired to study theology, and I was assigned to St. Meinrad. Ultimately, it worked out very well. While I wasn't geographically close to my grandmother and cousins, I was able to visit my godfather, who was a younger brother of my other grandmother, and I appreciated being in a rural area, which was great for bicycle riding and hiking. I studied at St. Meinrad for five academic years, earning the degrees of Master of Arts and Master of Divinity. The summers were for other pastoral experiences away from school.

I have only returned to "The Hill" twice in the past twenty-six years. I was planning to return in 2020 to join some of my classmates for our twenty-fifth anniversary, but our class reunion was canceled due to the coronavirus pandemic.

Although I never really discerned a monastic vocation, I greatly respect the monks. Diocesan priests may be asked to move to another parish on relatively short notice, but for monks, the monastery is a visible sign of their stability. Over the years, I have had the opportunity to join monastic communities on many occasions for an office of the Liturgy of the Hours or for a Mass, and I have always been mindful that I was participating in a prayer tradition that has continued for centuries. For example, at St. Meinrad, they have been praying on the same site for more than 150 years. Their prayers have continued even in times of fire, storms, and various hardships.

Every Benedictine monastery was founded by another one. St. Meinrad was founded by the Abbey of Einsiedeln in Switzerland, which has been in existence for over a thousand years and has a tradition of scholarship and missions. The study of letters, printing, and music greatly flourished there, and the abbey has contributed greatly to the Family of God, the Church. The monks came from Switzerland to Indiana to serve the German speaking immigrants who had settled in the rural region.

Entering a Benedictine abbey puts one in touch with St. Benedict, the "patriarch of western monasticism." About 1,500 years ago, St. Benedict founded a monastery, and, in one sense, left the world for the spiritual life. The Order that he founded, however, became instrumental in evangelization throughout Europe and helped in the preservation of culture in the so-called "Dark Ages." The monasteries became Christian centers of study, liturgy, architecture, and agriculture. The insignia and motto of St. Benedict includes the plough and the cross and the words *Ora et labora*, meaning Prayer and Work. Both are important, but prayer always comes first.

In my own diocese, we are fortunate to have Benedictine monks who follow the ancient Rule of Benedict. Belmont Abbey was founded in 1876 and has been a center of learning and ministry throughout these years. The first abbot served as the bishop of this area as the abbey preceded the formation of the Dioceses of Raleigh and Charlotte, and the monks of Belmont Abbey founded and staffed many parishes in North Carolina, including my own home parish in Salisbury.

As a seminarian, I spent two weeks at Belmont Abbey working on a project, and I was present several years ago when the abbey church received the honorary title of basilica. It is a title that the Holy Father may grant to a church building where there has been faithful service to God for many years and in recognition of significant art and architecture. At the abbey, there is a Blessed Sacrament chapel with Adoration of Blessed Sacrament. There is also a beautiful grotto on the grounds, which was modeled after the grotto of Lourdes where the Blessed Mother appeared to St. Bernadette in 1858.

I was impressed the first time that I went to Belmont Abbey almost fifty ago with my dad for a father-son retreat, and I still enjoy going over to the abbey with its beautiful campus for a visit, a walk, or a time of prayer. Every time that I visit the abbey, I am greeted with gracious hospitality, and I know that I have been enriched by my studies and visits among the Benedictines at St. Meinrad Seminary in Indiana, at Belmont Abbey, and at the other abbeys that I have visited over the years. I have come to admire the brothers and priests who serve the Lord and the Church as monks, and I am grateful that we have monasteries for retreats, spiritual direction, education, and prayer.

St. Benedict wrote, "Place nothing before the love of Christ." That is true sanctity.

St. Benedict, Please pray for us.

CHAPTER 37

Pope St. John XXIII: Pastor of Souls

He said to them, "The kings of the Gentiles lord
it over them and those in authority over them are
addressed as 'Benefactors' but among you it shall not
be so. Rather, let the greatest among you be as the
youngest, and the leader as the servant.
—LUKE 22:25-

The Second Vatican Council (1962–1965) was the most significant Catholic event of the last century, and many would agree that the council documents have yet to reach their full impact. I have found it very interesting to learn about the life and ministry of Pope St. John XXIII who convened the council and was pope at the time of my birth. Some would say that his papacy was unlikely based on his humble roots. St. John XXIII was born Angelo Giuseppe Roncalli in 1881 at Sotto il Monte, Italy, where his family worked as sharecroppers. He was the fourth child in a family of fourteen, and he grew up in a fervent religious atmosphere of his family and his parish. He entered the minor seminary at a young age and began the practice of making spiritual notes, which he continued in one form or another until his death. These notes have been gathered together in the text *Journal of a Soul*. He was ordained to the priesthood in 1904, and, as a young priest, he served as his bishop's secretary. Upon his bishop's death, he taught in the seminary and was involved in various pastoral ministries. During World War I, Fr. Roncalli served as a chaplain to wounded soldiers. In 1925, he was ordained a bishop and served as a diplomat for the Holy See in Bulgaria. He also served as an Apostolic Delegate in Turkey and Greece.

In December of 1944, Pius XII appointed him as the nuncio (the papal representative) in France. As a Vatican diplomat, his approach was always characterized by striving for Gospel simplicity, even amid the most complex diplomatic situations. The sincere piety of his interior life found expression each day in his prolonged periods of prayer and meditation. In 1953, he received the red hat as a cardinal and was sent to Venice as the archbishop and patriarch.

Upon his arrival in Venice, the new cardinal made the following statement:

> "The priest? From the day I was born, I thought of nothing else than to become a priest. Thus was a humble son of the people installed in the admirable office which redounds to the benefit of the people. The priest is there for the comfort and enlightenment of souls. He can discharge this function because he himself bears the weight of human frailty. As you look at your Patriarch, look for the priest, the minister of grace and look for naught else. The pastor? A little man, a humble priest, but above all a shepherd. As a young priest, my only aspiration was to become a country priest. . . . I will try quickly and silently, to put myself in touch with all of you, but in a simple and not in solemn way, and in the manner of the shepherd who counts his sheep one by one."[3]

He was filled with joy at the prospect of serving the remainder of his days as the pastor of souls in Venice. Five years later, however, Cardinal Roncalli was elected to the Chair of Peter at the age of seventy-seven, about fifty-four years after his ordination to the priesthood. St. John XXIII's pontificate lasted less than five years. During that time, he was seen throughout the world as an image of the Good Shepherd—meek and gentle, yet enterprising and courageous. He carried out his Chris-

---

[3] Henri Fesquet, *Wit and Wisdom of Good Pope* (New York: Signet Book, 1965), p. 108-109.

tian duties and exercised the corporal and spiritual works of mercy throughout the Diocese of Rome.

At his beatification in 2000, Pope St. John Paul II noted:

> *Everyone remembers the image of Pope John's smiling face and two outstretched arms embracing the whole world. How many people were won over by his simplicity of heart, combined with a broad experience of people and things! . . . his style of speaking and acting was new, as was his friendly approach to ordinary people and to the powerful of the world. It was in this spirit that he called the Second Vatican Ecumenical Council, thereby turning a new page in the Church's history: Christians heard themselves called to proclaim the Gospel with renewed courage and greater attentiveness to the "signs" of the times. The Council was a truly prophetic insight of this elderly Pontiff who, even amid many difficulties, opened a season of hope for Christians and for humanity. In the last moments of his earthly life, he entrusted his testament to the Church: "What counts the most in life is blessed Jesus Christ, his holy Church, his Gospel, truth and goodness." We too wish to receive this testament, as we glorify God for having given him to us as a Pastor.*

Pope St. John XXIII was faithful until the end of his life.

CHAPTER 38

Mission Societies and a Return to the Nunciature

The generation to come will be told of the Lord,
that they may proclaim to a people yet unborn the
deliverance you have brought.
—PSALM 22:32

Many diocesan priests serve as the pastor or parochial vicar of a parish and also have other responsibilities such as being a chaplain or teacher for a Catholic school or working in a seminary or in a diocesan office such as the tribunal. In addition to pastoral ministry, I have served on our vocations committee and was also appointed as the diocesan director for the Pontifical Mission Societies for a five-year term. After only two years as diocesan director, I was invited by the national director to serve on the national board, which involved participation in additional meetings and events. The national board advises the national director on the budget, policies, and priorities of the mission societies. The national director has a huge responsibility as millions of dollars pass through the national office to the Vatican Congregation for the Evangelization of Peoples and to mission projects throughout the world. The Catholics of the United States have been very charitable to the world's missions over the years.

As diocesan director, one of my tasks was to promote World Mission Sunday, which is celebrated every October. A goal of World Mission Sunday includes a call to all dioceses and parishes to recognize their common responsibility in regard to evangelization to the peoples of the world. It is an invitation to see beyond the local needs and concerns and to support missions throughout the Church through prayer and sacrifice. The dioceses of Raleigh and Charlotte have a history of being in the missions. At one time, North Carolina was the least Catholic state in the United States by percentage of the overall population.

In the Decree on the Church's Missionary Activity of Vatican II, it was noted that "the Church on earth is by its very nature missionary since, according to the plan of the Father, it has its origin in the mission of the Son and the Holy Spirit" (no. 2). We believe that Christ is the answer for a troubled world, and missionaries joyfully share the Gospel message of hope. World Mission Sunday is an invitation to recommit ourselves to bringing the Gospel to others.

The Lord sent his Apostles out to make disciples and to proclaim the Good News. Visiting the missions is something that I encourage, and I have received many blessings on mission trips to Jamaica, the Dominican Republic, and Peru. Our nation has many material resources in comparison to some of the mission territories, and the collection on World Mission Sunday helps with their material needs—building chapels and clinics, providing catechetical books, and covering the cost to train seminarians. The human connection with others in mission areas in the Church has certainly enriched my life and priestly ministry.

During my term as diocesan director and as a member of the national board, I was in contact with missionaries throughout the world, usually by phone, mail, or e-mail. While these mission priests and bishops serve in different parts of the world, they all shared their joy of priestly ministry in serving the Lord and the faithful.

In 2012, in our board meeting in Washington, D.C., we were blessed by the presence of Archbishop Savio Hon Tai-Fai, S.D.B., Secretary of the Vatican Congregation for the Evangelization of Peoples. Archbishop Hon was born in Hong Kong where he was educated by the Salesians. He entered the order at the age of twelve and eventually became their provincial. He was responsible for the translation of the *Catechism of the Catholic Church* into Chinese, and, two years later, he was asked to serve in the Vatican where he was ordained an archbishop. He gave our board an interesting perspective on the situation of the Catholic Church in China. He noted that while there is not full religious liberty, there are, however, many conversions. For example, he noted that in one parish in China there were 220 people in RCIA the previous year. I haven't ever heard of numbers like that around here!

Another positive experience of our board meeting was a reception at the Apostolic Nunciature, which is the residence of the Apostolic Nuncio, the Vatican's Ambassador to the United States. The Holy See has ambassadors in about 100 nations and some diplomatic interaction with an additional sixty nations. The nuncio serves as a liaison between the Holy Father and the government of the United States. He also announces the appointment of new bishops and usually attends their ordinations or installations. The Vatican has appointed diplomatic delegates to the U.S. since 1893. The nuncio, at that time, was Archbishop Carlo Maria Viganò, and he was a gracious host to our group.

As I received my elegant invitation to the formal reception at the nunciature, I had to smile. I had been there once before, about twenty years earlier. At that time, I was a somewhat ignorant seminarian. In fact, I knew very little about a lot of things. During a school break, I had traveled to Washington, D.C., to visit my grandmother, and, somehow, I had heard about an apostolic nuncio living in Washington, D.C., who was pope's representative. I decided to call the nunciature and inquire if they offered tours of their facility. The phone number was in the phone book, and so I just called. I thought that they might have a small museum or a visitation area. I admit that I was truly a greenhorn and didn't even understand that the nunciature is the equivalent of an embassy! A priest from the Diocese of Brooklyn, a diplomatic secretary, took my call. After I made my inquiry about tours, he responded loudly with a perfect Brooklyn accent, "Tours? No, we don't have any tours!!" I told him that I was sorry and that I was a seminarian in town to visit my grandmother, and I was just curious. He lowered his voice and said that the nuncio, Archbishop Cacciavillan, was away, and so the house was less stressful. He then invited me to come over for a visit. I quickly accepted his offer.

I looked up the address and, on my way over, I passed many elegant embassies in the neighborhood. I parked my old clunker right out front, and the priest was very gracious with me after I arrived at the main door. We sat in the parlor, and one of the sisters on the staff brought us tea and cookies. Father showed me around a little, we chatted a bit, and then I went on my way, thankful for the experience. I have never heard of another seminarian who had been treated with tea and cookies at the nunciature!

So, after about twenty years, I was able to return to the nunciature as a member of the National Board of Directors of the Pontifical Mission Societies of the United States. This time, I had an official and elaborate invitation, which I proudly showed to the priests serving as diplomatic secretaries! I still have it somewhere. It was a fun return and for the official reception, we were given more than just tea and cookies. It was a grand catered spread. Archbishop Carlo Maria Viganò, who has been in the news in recent years, was very welcoming to our group that evening, and I even received an official photo standing beside him at the top of the beautiful staircase.

Another great experience during my time on the board was the Venerable Fulton J. Sheen World Mission Dinner some years ago on October 1 at the Pierre Hotel in Manhattan. While it was admittedly a very elegant setting with a $1,000 per plate offering, it was certainly all for a great cause—to raise money for scholarships for religious sisters from mission countries. October 1 is the Memorial of St. Thérèse of the Child Jesus, "The Little Flower," who with St. Francis Xavier is the co-patroness of the missions. She is a Doctor of the Church, and we were fortunate to have her small writing desk at the dinner. It was on this small drawer desk that she wrote *The Story of a Soul.* Shortly after it was published, it was translated into numerous languages and has inspired many faithful Christians for the past one hundred years. In her book, she wrote that she came to the

Carmel "to save souls and to pray for priests." The dinner was named for the late Archbishop Fulton J. Sheen, who was the director of the Society for the Propagation of the Faith from 1950 to 1966. Venerable Fulton Sheen, who had a positive impact on the world through his television and radio shows, his books, his travels, and his homilies, taught that the Church is missionary by her very nature.

On my last trip to Rome, I had the honor of meeting some of the mission sisters living in Castel Gandolfo near Rome, who represented some forty nations. After their studies, they will return to their home countries to be leaders especially with Church ministries, education, and works of mercy. It was an honor to participate.

We know that all of the baptized share in the continued mission of the Church, and it is important to support the missions with our presence, our financial and material donations, and our prayers.

Everyone has something to learn and something to share.

With Archbishop Hon of the Vatican Congregation for the Evangelization of Peoples after a Mass in the Basilica Shrine of the Immaculate Conception in Washington, D.C., 2012

CHAPTER 39

Mission Trips

After Barnabas and Saul completed their relief mission, they returned to Jerusalem, taking with them John, who is called Mark.
—ACTS 12:25

A few people have asked me about mission trips over the years. In fact, one of my brothers even asked me shortly after I returned from Peru, "What was the purpose of your trip?" Here is a brief reflection on some of my four mission experiences in Peru in which we helped their missions by providing construction materials, liturgical items, catechetical books, Bibles, and funding for parish projects. However, as important as these things are, mission trips are more about making connections with people, our brothers and sisters in the Faith.

I traveled to Peru for the first time in the summer of 2006. On that trip, I first visited the historic sites in Cusco and Machu Picchu. I was truly impressed with that area, especially with the Inca stonework. It is in the high Andes in the south of the country. I then met one of my parishioners from Charlotte, Luis, a native of Peru for the next phase of the trip, which was to visit the jungle region, where he had worked some years earlier as an engineer. We met some of the priests and sisters working in the Apostolic Vicariate of Pucallpa. The vicariate was in the process of building a pastoral center in the Parish of St. Martin in Aguaytía. Upon my return to Charlotte, we had a special collection in the parish that helped to complete and furnish the pastoral center. After welcoming to our parish two priests serving in the jungle region the following year, we had another collection that supported the construction materials for a chapel in the community of Neshuya. We also provided some funds to help a few projects, including the reconstruction of a parish church that had to be rebuilt following an earthquake.

One of the highlights of the trip was a visit to the small mission of Tournavista on the Pachitea River. I remember that it was like going to the end of the earth! There were four sisters and four postulants living in what appeared to be an old primitive farmhouse. They did not have running water or a phone. As they only had electricity for two and a half hours per day, they had no refrigeration. They used a small gas burner for cooking, and the sisters and postulants hauled water from a community well for cooking and washing, and they all shared a very rustic outhouse, which was basically a hole in the ground surrounded by rough walls. My heart was moved by their humble quarters and their Christian joy. They prepared a great meal for us of fish and potatoes using their small gas burner and a skillet.

I promised on the spot to help provide a well, a water tank, and a pump for the sister's humble convent. The sisters visit fifty-two native communities along the rivers. They travel in small, open, motorized canoes and often sleep in the jungle. It is certainly not a luxury cruise as the canoe seats do not even have a backrest and the rivers are not for swimming as they are full of piranhas. It takes them two to three days to reach some of the more distant communities.

The Vicariate of Pucallpa is an enormous pastoral territory. At the time of my visit, there were about twenty-five priests and about thirty sisters ministering to roughly five hundred communities. They rely a lot on the ministry of lay catechists to teach the Faith in some of the outlying communities. Some of the priests and sisters visit communities that are only accessible by boat, and it takes that bishop about four days to visit some of the most remote communities. I was again amazed at how much they accomplish with relatively meager material resources and very little help from outside their region. I know that while their ministry is in many ways different than the pastoral ministry in my own home diocese, there is a bond that we all share by virtue of our Baptism and Faith.

Some of my great memories of the trips include participating in a large healing Mass, the day Fr. Gregory and I baptized some seventy persons, visiting the island community of Masisea —a community located about two and a half hours away by boat from Pucallpa—celebrating Mass in the cathedral of Pucallpa, visiting various ministries in Huánuco, and celebrating Mass in the Cathedral of Callao, which is in the major port of the capital city of Lima.

On one trip to Peru, a priest of the cathedral of Huánuco invited me to join him for an early morning Mass for a group of children at a Salesian youth center. On the walk from the cathedral to the youth center, he asked if I would preside and preach. I was truly not prepared to preach in Spanish and was a little nervous as we arrived. We entered though a back door of the chapel and then vested for the early Mass. When we entered the narrow chapel, we were greeted by the joyful singing voices of some 300 poor children. The experience touched me so profoundly that I could barely speak to begin the Mass.

Another highlight was celebrating the Solemnity of St. Rose of Lima (a national holiday) in three different communities and baptizing ten children in a small rural chapel with an earthen floor. St. Rose is the first canonized saint of the new world and a patroness of the Americas.

Before I left Tournavista, I promised the sisters, who were basically beating a clump of scrap metal for the mission bell, that we would provide a mission bell for the chapel, and I promised that I would return again to ring it.

My life has been enriched by my time among the faithful in Peru.

With Salesian Sister Anita and youth

With Bishop Jaime, Luis, and Padre Juan at the cathedral in Huánuco

CHAPTER 40

The Holy Land

*For the peace of Jerusalem pray: "May those who
love you prosper! May peace be within your ram-
parts, prosperity within your towers.*
PSALM 122:6-7

It was a blessing to have been invited by Gail Buckley of
Catholic Scripture Study, Inc., to serve as a chaplain for a
Holy Land Pilgrimage in 2009. It was also a blessing to be
in the company of the hosts and guides Steve and Janet Ray,
who have a great knowledge of the Holy Land and are enthusiastic Catholic witnesses.

A pilgrimage to the Holy Land affords one an opportunity
to see and experience the places that are important in Scripture
and in Salvation History. I knew that it would be an enriching
experience with regard to teaching and preaching, but a pilgrimage also renews one's spiritual life. Seeing sites that have
been venerated by countless pilgrims reminded me that the
Church, as the Family of God, transcends time.

Among the great memories were trips to Bethlehem, Nazareth, Mt. Tabor, the Mount of Beatitudes, Capernaum, Cana,
Caesarea Philippi, and, of course, Jerusalem. People have asked
if there was a high point for me. It was all great, but the opportunities to lead the Way of the Cross along the traditional
stations and to celebrate the Mass at the Tomb of Christ were
the high points for me.

I was able to visit the Church of the Holy Sepulcher, which
encloses the last few stations, Calvary, and the empty tomb,
several times. The Upper Room is the site of the institution of

the Holy Eucharist and the Christian Priesthood, and the place where the disciples received the Holy Spirit on Pentecost. That room also became a special place of prayer for all of us. Steve Ray told us that, after a pilgrimage to the Holy Land, Christmas and Holy Week will always be different.

That has certainly proved to be true.

Mass at the Lord's tomb in Jerusalem in 2009

CHAPTER 41

Parish History and Connections

What thanksgiving, then, can we render to God for
you, for all the joy we feel on your account before
our God?
—1 THES 3:9

O
ne of the things that I remember hearing in the seminary was the importance of learning the parish history of where one is assigned. A diocesan priest on the faculty at the seminary once remarked to our class, "Remember that there were people in that parish before you arrived and there will be people in that parish after you leave!" Another thing that I have learned as a pastor is that parishioners remember their former pastors and often compare their strengths and weaknesses. As I have learned the history of each parish where I have served, I am reminded of Divine Providence.

In 1961, just before I was born, Bishop Vincent Waters of Raleigh purchased about eight acres on a dirt road known as Old Reid in Charlotte. The diocese recognized that there were going to be new homes built in the area and considered putting a school and a parish on the site, and a gym was first constructed to serve as a temporary chapel. Msgr. Michael J. Begley was the pastor of St. Ann's when Bishop Waters purchased the property for St. Vincent's Mission Chapel and had the initial responsibility for the pastoral care of the souls of the new mission. Msgr. Begley became the first Bishop of the Diocese of Charlotte in January of 1972. Shortly after my twelfth birthday the following year, I met Bishop Begley for the first time at my

Confirmation. At that time, I certainly never imagined that in one aspect, I would follow his pastoral ministry at the Parish of St. Vincent de Paul. Forty-two years after the first Mass was celebrated at St. Vincent's in 1961, I was appointed the pastor of a thriving parish where I would serve for fourteen years.

I met Fr. Joe Waters shortly after my ordination. He was one of our tireless priests, often traveling to different parishes and missions every weekend to celebrate Masses and sacraments mostly in Spanish. He was known to be very humble and charitable. I even heard that once he gave his bed from the rectory to a poor person. He stayed active as long as he could. Fr. Joe had been celebrating the Spanish Masses in Jefferson and at the mission in Sparta as a "circuit rider" for several years at the time that I moved there from Biscoe in 1999.

When I arrived, he simply moved on to help in another parish. After I was appointed to St. Vincent de Paul in Charlotte in 2003, I learned that Fr. Waters had been the pastor there almost thirty years earlier. Finally, after I was appointed pastor in Mooresville, I again was pleased to learn that Fr. Joe Waters had served as the pastor here more than fifty years earlier! Now deceased, people still remember the faithfulness and pastoral care of Fr. Joe Waters.

I was pleased that I became friends with another former pastor of St. Vincent de Paul, Msgr. John Roueche, in his retirement in Southern Pines. In a way, I also followed in the footsteps of Msgr. Roueche, who was pastor there from 1971 to 1973 and is remembered in a pictorial directory as "a kindly and zealous priest." He was from Salisbury and was a descendent of the first Catholic family, some of whom are still parishioners. He was also the first priest from my home parish of Sacred Heart, where he was ordained to the priesthood in 1933. Sixty-one years later, I entered Holy Orders with my diaconate ordination at Sacred Heart. There were a couple of people who were at both ordinations sixty-one years apart. I have been fortunate to have followed fine pastors in my priestly assignments. Let us continue the path of "faithful service" to God and to the Family of God, the Church. I remain thankful for the pastoral witness of my predecessors.

May the faithful departed, especially Bishop Begley, Fr Joe Waters and Msgr. Roueche, rest in peace.

CHAPTER 42

Remembering Uncle Fred

*Remember the deeds that our ancestors did in their
times, and you shall win great honor and an everlasting name.*
—1 MC 2:51

While reflecting on the Sacrament of Baptism, I also reflect on the role of godparents and my own godfather, Uncle Fred, who was one of my grandmother's brothers. I never knew my Uncle Fred very well until I went to the seminary. He always lived far away from us and, prior to my time in the seminary, my only memory of him and his wife, Elsie, my godmother, was at a family reunion on Long Island when I was seventeen years old. My grandmother sometimes called him by his birth name, Carmine. I asked him once, "Uncle Fred, why did you change your name?" He responded that, in the 1930's, it seemed that about every other Mafia hitman that was brought in was named Carmine.

Bishop Donoghue sent me to study at St. Meinrad Seminary in Southern Indiana in 1990, and my uncle lived in Louisville, Kentucky, only about eighty miles away. I got his phone number from my father and called him up, and we got reacquainted. We actually became very close friends, and I would often escape from the seminary for a weekend to visit my Uncle Fred. Sometimes, we would play a round of golf, go out to dinner, or simply watch television. I would also help him with projects or repairs around the house. My Aunt Elsie had already passed away, and Uncle Fred lived alone. We were about fifty years different in age. In his eighties, he was still very active in his parish, and he helped to serve drinks at various parish dinners. I was so pleased that he was able to participate in my ordinations to the diaconate and to the priesthood. He was a quiet person of sincere faith. As I had very little contact with him until I was almost thirty, I was very proud to see him active in his parish.

One thing that I remember clearly was that sometimes after a nice dinner or a nice round of golf, he would say, "My cup runneth over." Of course, that line from the twenty-third Psalm refers to the cup of blessings. I say it now quite often myself as I am aware of my many blessings.

He told me the story of his faith. His father had a bit of a temper, and, when he was about seven or eight years old, his father got into an argument with their pastor on the front porch of the church. His father finally told the priest with his hand raised, "You will never see me here again or any of my children!" Fred said that his initial reaction was, "Hurray! We don't have go to church anymore." He said, however, that as he grew up, every time that he passed a Catholic Church (and there are many of them in Queens), he felt a draw or a pull. He said that it was like "The Hound of Heaven" poem by Francis Thompson. I had never heard of that poem before then, but I looked it up in the seminary library. Amazingly, Fred took instructions for confirmation in another parish and was confirmed there without any of his family members present. And, of the six children, I think that they all found their way back to the Church in one way or another.

Uncle Fred was called from this life in 1999. I am thankful for his role as my godfather and as a close friend. He stood with me at my baptism, and he also stood with me at my ordination as a deacon. Interestingly, Uncle Fred was also my father's godfather in 1935.

The tradition of the Church is that each person must have at least one baptismal sponsor, although most have two. At least one godparent is to be a confirmed and active Catholic living in harmony with the teachings of the Church and be at least sixteen years old. The godparent is entering into a spiritual relationship with the person being baptized.

Baptism is the beginning of a life of grace. It is a spiritual rebirth and the first Sacrament of Initiation. There are two major benefits from Baptism. First, it washes away Original Sin. This is the sin that all have inherited through human generation since the first couple, Adam and Eve, chose to disobey God. The second benefit of Baptism is that it incorporates one into the Family of God, the Church, which is the Mystical Body of Christ.

Baptism is thus a joyful sacrament.

With my Godfather, Uncle Fred, just before my diaconate ordination

CHAPTER 43

Priests and Heroes

*Know that the LORD works wonders for his faithful
one; the LORD hears when I call out to him.*
—PSALM 4:4

S omeone just recently asked me if there were priests who
inspired me during my time of discernment. Certainly,
I admired the pastoral care of some of the parish priests
that I knew from my home parish in Salisbury and from our
diocese. I was also impressed with some of the priests that I met
in the Diocese of Charleston, where I first heard the call of the
Lord. I was also inspired by the priestly witness of saints that I
had read about. The source for the following is from the book,
The Cure of Ars: The Priest Who Out-Talked the Devil by Milton
Lomask.

St. John Mary Vianney was a true example of a pastor at
the service of Christ's flock. During the Year for Priests in 2009,
Pope Benedict XVI proclaimed St. John Vianney as the patron
saint of all priests, not only parish priests. At the time, the Holy
Father encouraged all priests to seek an interior renewal for
their personal sanctity and priestly witness to the Gospel in the
world. "Priests," the pontiff said, "should look to the life and
ministry of St. John Vianney."

As a young boy of only five years old, St. John saw great
terror and violence during the French Revolution. Many Catholic priests and religious were murdered or exiled during this
dark period, and his own parish was closed. Two years later, he
met a holy priest and received his father's permission to study

at the seminary to begin his formation. Although never an outstanding student, he persevered and was eventually ordained a priest in 1815 at the age of twenty-nine. Three years later he was named the parish priest of Ars. As he received his assignment, the bishop told him that the parish of Ars had about 200 souls, and that the parish church was in bad repair. He noted that "there is very little love of God in Ars and that his job would be to put some in it."

Upon his arrival, the new pastor learned that only a few little children had been baptized and that about seventy-five percent of the older ones had not been confirmed. Very few had received any religious instruction. Starting with about four faithful families, the whole parish was gradually transformed. As a preacher, confessor, and director of souls, St. John Vianney became known throughout the whole region and beyond. His life was one of extreme mortification as he only slept two or three hours per day and survived with minimal sustenance. At times, he heard confessions for up to sixteen hours per day! His life was filled with works of charity and pastoral care. It is recorded that even the staunchest of sinners were converted in his presence. I heard in the seminary, although I have never seen it in print, that St. John Vianney was the catalyst for the round-trip ticket. Many people in France wanted to go to confession in Ars, but they didn't plan to stay around. They therefore requested to book their return train ticket so they could make their confession and then return home. It is an interesting story!

He was also a person of great humility. Out of jealousy for his popularity, a neighboring pastor once sought to have him removed and circulated a petition to be sent to the bishop with the headline: "Fr. John Vianney is an ignorant fool." A shocked parishioner brought a copy of the petition to St. John, who upon reading it, promptly signed it! Now that is a example of humility!

He served in Ars for forty-two years and was totally dedicated to his priestly ministry. He opened a school for poor girls and gave daily catechism lessons. He died at the age of seventy-four, peacefully and without fear. He remains to this day the living image of the priest after the heart of Christ. He recognized that the priesthood is the love of the heart of Jesus and that priests serve in the Person of Christ in the sacraments. He was a true pastor of souls and a model for those of us in ministry.

I was inspired after I saw the movie *The Mission* about the Jesuit missions in South America. After the movie, I read about the founder of the Society of Jesus, St. Ignatius of Loyola. It is a great story. Ignatius was trained for a military career, but it came to an abrupt end when, during a battle, a cannonball shattered some bones in his leg. It was during his long convalescence that he read *The Life of Christ* and a collection of the lives of the saints. After several years of study, Ignatius gathered six companions who vowed to live in poverty and chastity and to preach the Gospel to the nations. He developed the Spiritual Exercises that are still used throughout the world. At the time of his death in 1540, the Society numbered 1,000 members, some of whom were already serving in foreign missions. The motto of the Jesuits is *ad maiorem Dei gloriam* (to the greater Glory of God). St. Ignatius is the patron saint of soldiers and retreatants, which I have always thought was a great combination. There are patron saints of soldiers and others for retreatants, but he is a patron saint for both.

I think that it was my grandmother who first told me about Fr. Damien, the leper priest. While I was a seminarian, I read several books about the ministry of Fr. Damien on the Island of Molokai, which greatly inspired me. At the time of his canonization in October of 2009, Pope Benedict XVI preached about St. Damien's faithful ministry among the sick and dying in the Hawaiian Islands, which are located very far from his native Belgium. He volunteered for the missions and then volunteered to be the chaplain for the leper community. Additionally, he became their nurse, their carpenter, their advocate, and their friend. St. Damien was a true missionary who joyfully proclaimed and lived the Gospel of Jesus. In his constant service to the sick, St. Damian contacted the dreaded disease that took his life. He is a martyr of compassion and charity, who gave his life in the service of others.

St. Vincent de Paul's name is synonymous with charitable activities on behalf of the poor. Vincent de Paul was born in 1581 in a relatively poor family. He became a young priest at the age of nineteen and was captured by pirates while on a sea voyage. He spent two years in captivity and succeeded in converting his master to Christianity. He then served in a parish and in various chaplaincies until he gathered together a group that would be the basis of the Congregation of the Mission, later known as the Vincentians. This group of priests and brothers engaged in parish missions among the poor and uneducated. In 1633, together with St. Louise de Marillac, St. Vincent de Paul founded a congregation of religious women known as the Daughters of Charity. Their apostolate was in social work and charity. St. Vincent also served in the formation of the clergy by founding a seminary. Fr. Vincent's generosity and goodness attracted many people, and he left a positive impact in his native France. He died in the autumn of 1660 after about sixty years in the priesthood. He was canonized by Pope Clement XII in 1737, and Pope Leo XIII named him patron of all charitable works throughout the Catholic world. I was pleased to pray in the chapel where his body rests in Paris.

In the Office of Readings of the Liturgy of the Hours, we have the following excerpt from a writing of St. Vincent de Paul, who wrote:

> *We must take care of the poor, console them, help them, support their cause. Since Christ willed to be poor, He chose for Himself disciples who were poor. He made Himself the servant of the poor and shared their poverty. He went so far as to say that He would consider every deed which either helps or harms the poor as done for or against Himself. Since God surely loves the poor, He also loves those who love the poor.*

A couple of great books about St. Vincent de Paul include: *St. Vincent de Paul* by F. A. Forbes (available through TAN books) and *Vincent de Paul: Saint of Charity* by Margaret Ann Hubbard.

Although not a priest, but a faithful deacon, St. Francis of Assisi remains among the best known and admired of the canonized saints. Statues of him may be found in parishes, monasteries, gardens, and yards throughout the world. The prayer attributed to him is often invoked in speeches at the United Nations: "Lord, make me an instrument of your peace." He was honored by the U.S. Postal Service when a commemorative stamp was issued in 1982 on the 800th anniversary of his birth. Franciscan priests, brothers, sisters, Third Order Religious, and Secular Franciscans serve in missions, schools, and parishes throughout the Church. Franciscans are the custodians of the holy sites of the Holy Land and were the founders of the California Missions. All of this follows the faithful ministry of the son of a cloth merchant who was born in a small village in Italy long ago.

St. Francis was one who desired to conform his life to Christ. He was certainly not looking for personal fame or recognition. After a couple of failed experiences in military service, he heard the call of the Lord "to repair the Church which was falling into ruins." He initially thought the call referred to the small pilgrim's chapel, St. Damian, which was in need of repairs. He gathered together a small group with the intention of preaching and teaching while living in poverty and humility. When it became time for them to seek papal approval for their new religious order, Francis and his eleven followers walked to Rome to seek an audience with Pope Innocent III. After several days, the Holy Father agreed to meet with the brothers. In those days, it was very rare for the pope to approve a new order at the first meeting. The pope, however, recognized Francis from a dream that he had had in which he saw Francis holding up the Basilica of St. John Lateran, the cathedral church of Rome and mother church of Christendom. With papal approval, the new order grew and, before long, they were preaching throughout Italy and in foreign nations. St. Francis expressed a spirituality of humility, simplicity, and purity.

From the Liturgy of the Hours for his memorial on October 4th: "Francis left this earth a poor and lowly man; he entered Heaven rich in God's favor, greeted with songs of rejoicing."

Saints are those members of the Mystical Body of Christ of the Church Triumphant. They are close to the Lord. Their lives are remembered for holiness and virtue.

We should all be mindful of the lives of the saints, especially those that we have been named after and the patron saint of our parishes.

CHAPTER 44

The Rite of Christian Initiation of Adults

Do not delay turning back to the LORD,
do not put it off day after day.
—SIRACH 5:7

The word conversion comes from the classical Latin *converto,* which means "change." In the Christian sense, conversion refers to a spiritual change or enlightenment. It may even entail "a return to God." We acknowledge the gift of grace in the conversion process. God initiates the relationship and invites a response. Many people pray for the conversion of family members, friends, and co-workers. St. Monica is a model of prayer as she prayed many years and shed many tears for the conversion of her son, St. Augustine. For many, conversion is an initial step toward an investigation and examination of the teachings of the Church.

One of my grandmothers told me that when my grandfather, Bill Test, who was an American Baptist, proposed to her, she told him that she was not really interested in entering a "mixed marriage." Some of her friends who were in such marriages were experiencing some religious stress. In her nineties, she told me that she later regretted giving him an ultimatum. It is perhaps better not to push one in the spiritual life. Bill knew that his girlfriend was strong in her Catholic Faith and that she was not planning to change. He did, however, have many sincere questions about Catholicism, and, when he asked these to my grandmother, she responded, "I believe my Faith, but I am not able to respond to each of your questions." She then suggested that they go to the Dominican House of Studies in Washington, D.C., to speak with a priest. They did, and a priest greeted them. While "Madge" waited in the lobby, Bill went into an office and spoke with the priest. She told me that when they returned to the lobby, the priest remarked, "Mr. Test certainly knows the Scriptures very well." Bill was also satisfied with the answers that he received from the Dominican. He took instructions in a parish and was received into the fullness of the Catholic Church prior to their Nuptial Mass in 1933. I have no idea who that priest was, but when I visited the Dominican House in Washington more than seventy years later, I thanked them for their faithfulness and for their part in my grandfather's spiritual journey many years earlier. We have the gift of reason, and I think that it is reasonable to believe, and yet faith as a divine virtue is beyond an intellectual conviction. There is no pressure, and we have welcomed many spouses into our RCIA program, sometimes many years after their marriage and participation in the Holy Mass.

When I was the pastor in Jefferson, North Carolina, I met a faithful couple in the parish. The wife was from Louisiana, and the husband was from a Baptist family but had never been baptized. They were charter members of the parish and were at Mass every Sunday with their family. The husband requested Baptism and the Sacraments of Initiation on their fiftieth wedding anniversary. He had been attending the Catholic Mass consistently for fifty years! The wife told me that she never pressured him.

I have directed the RCIA programs in the parishes where I have been the pastor. It is the Lord who inspires conversions, and we are but instruments of His initiative. Every year, I have met people who are seeking the truth. Some are spouses of Catholics, some are engaged, and others have come following the Christian witness of neighbors, friends, and co-workers. I have met some who have actually read their way into Catholicism. It is joyful for me to meet new candidates for the Sacraments of Initiation every year. It demonstrates that the local Church is alive.

RCIA is among my great joys in pastoral ministry. It is a

period of discernment, prayer, and study in which the Church instructs and then receives new adult members. At Easter, some will receive the fullness of Catholic Initiation with the celebration of the Sacraments of Baptism, Confirmation, and Eucharist, while those who have already been validly baptized will receive the sacraments of Penance, Confirmation, and the Holy Eucharist. There is always joy when an adult comes to the reality that our Church is the Mystical Body of Christ and the Family of God. Within the Catholic Church, we find the fullness of the Faith. The sacraments are for us the channels of sanctifying grace and the stepping stones to eternal life. While hundreds are received into the fullness of the Faith in our diocese every year, perhaps more than one million are received into the Church throughout the world.

We should note, however, that all are called to an ongoing conversion. We should turn from sin and turn to the Lord. In an Angelus message during the Octave of Easter some years ago, Pope Benedict XVI said the following regarding our Christian responsibility:

> *Dear friends, Yes, Christ is truly risen! We cannot keep for ourselves the life and joy that He has given us in His Passover, but rather we must give it to all who approach us. It is our duty and our mission: to kindle in the heart of our neighbor—hope where there is despair, joy where there is sorrow, life where there is death.*

Every year, a special community forms through the RCIA sessions, and there are many periods of grace. While the primary purpose of RCIA is to form and welcome new members, it has the added benefit of educating Catholics who desire to learn more.

It is a lifetime mission.

CHAPTER 45

Freedom and Responsibility

*For freedom Christ set us free; so stand firm and do
not submit again to the yoke of slavery.*
—GAL 5:1

O f course, there is a lot of news these days regarding the political process in the United States. I think that recent national elections certainly exhibit contrasting ideologies. The Church, while primarily concerned with the spiritual realm, is also involved with life in the temporal order. St. Paul wrote that while we are in the world, we should not be conformed to the world (see Rom 12:2). This is clear in the Church's social and moral teachings. The Church is universal and, therefore, exists in nations where there are different political systems. While the Church does not govern the political process, the members of the Church are encouraged to be involved in striving for the common good of all people. In nations where there exists a free vote, citizens are encouraged to prepare prior to voting by learning and reflecting on each candidate's positions, while being guided by faith, Scripture, reason, and the teachings of the Church.

Catholics have long served in the temporal order. The September 2011 edition of the Knights of Columbus's Columbia magazine included an article on the statesman Charles Carroll of Carrollton. As a delegate to the Continental Congress from Maryland, Charles Carroll was the only Catholic among the fifty-six signers of the Declaration of Independence, and he is remembered as an influential figure in the founding of the United States. While there existed in the colonies some anti-Catholic sentiments, Carroll was respected by the other founding fathers. He was well-educated and successful. His cousin, Archbishop John Carroll of Baltimore, was the first bishop of the United States. Charles Carroll served the new country in the Continental Congress, the U.S. Senate, and the Maryland Senate. He also helped draft the U.S. Constitution. Charles Carroll and the other signers of the Declaration of Independence were considered criminals, guilty of sedition against King George III upon their signing of the Declaration. They, therefore, were men of integrity who were willing to sacrifice for the sake of principle. We are all in debt to those who stood tall in the face of trials, and we honor the memories of those who have sacrificed to preserve these freedoms to our day.

While we may recognize shortcomings in our republic, travel outside of our borders may give us a perspective and remind us how much we have to be thankful for. The United States does prioritize many aspects in the realm of freedom for its citizens, although we are aware of intrusions into the freedom of the practice of religion, especially with regard to executive orders, health care mandates, and related issues. We should remember that with freedom comes responsibility.

Prior to future elections, let us take an interest and pursue the best path. I doubt that there will be a "perfect" candidate, but our participation in the process honors those such as Charles Carroll, who risked their lives, property, and status to establish these United States.

It is an opportunity to discern sacrifice and responsibility.

CHAPTER 46

Reflections on the Priesthood

If we live in the Spirit, let us also follow the Spirit.
—GAL 5:25

I am sometimes asked what I enjoy about being a priest and what aspects are challenging. First, I have to say that I am humbled and thankful that I was called to be a priest. When I graduated from college in 1983, I sincerely thought that I would be working in the field of engineering for my whole career. The great joy of a priest is in the celebration of the sacraments. We believe in the transforming power of grace. While celebrating Mass at the altar of sacrifice, and while absolving sins in the confessional, the priest is an instrument of God who acts in the Person of Christ. Every day, I look forward to the celebration of Mass and praying the Liturgy of the Hours, the Chaplet of Divine Mercy, and the Holy Rosary.

Around the time of the fiftieth anniversary of his ordination to the priesthood, Pope St. John Paul II offered this inspiring reflection:

> *I still remember with emotion, after the wait and preparation with prayer during the month of October, the rite of ordination by the archbishop of Krakow, Adam Stefan Sapieha, in his private chapel. Since then I have let myself be guided by the Lord along the paths that He has opened before me day after day: priestly ministry in the different areas of pastoral activity, responsibility for my diocese as Archbishop of Krakow, and later, the service of the Church in Rome as Successor of Peter. . . . Throughout these years I have always started my day with the celebration of the Eucharist, foundation and heart of*

163

my entire priestly life, discovering each time with immense gratitude that this is the mysterious and essential link that unites each priest with Christ the Redeemer. In the school of Jesus, Priest and Victim, I have understood better and better that the priest does not live for himself, but for the Church and for the sanctification of the People of God."

Pope St. John Paul II certainly gave all priests, religious, and faithful a great witness of mission, while remaining united to the Lord in the Blessed Sacrament.

The priest is called to bring a sense of hope to the critically ill and consolation to the grieving. It is never easy to counsel families who have suffered a great loss. We cannot explain God's plan, but we are able to trust in God's mercy. I think that the parish priest will only be effective if he is dedicated to prayer and the sacramental life, and Adoration is extremely helpful. Venerable Fulton J. Sheen made a Holy Hour every day during his life as a priest and bishop—more than sixty years! He wrote in his autobiography, *Treasure in Clay,* that he was sure that the Holy Hour had preserved his vocation.

He wrote:

"The purpose of the Holy Hour is to encourage deep personal encounter with Christ. The holy and glorious God is constantly inviting us to come to Him, to hold converse with Him, to ask for such things as we need and to experience what a blessing there is in fellowship with Him."

"So the Holy Hour, quite apart from all its positive spiritual benefits, kept my feet from wandering too far . . . The Holy Hour became like an oxygen tank to revive the breath of the Holy Spirit in the foul and fetid atmosphere of the world." [4]

---

[4] Fulton J. Sheen, *Treasure in Clay, The Autobiography of Fulton J. Sheen* (New York, Doubleday,1980), p. 190, p. 192.

All of the faithful are encouraged to pray the Rosary, but I think that it is especially important for priests. In this regard, Pope St. John Paul II encouraged a "daily rosary," as have other saints. When I was in the seminary, a group of seminarians would gather in the theology chapel to pray the Rosary at 9 pm. One of the seminarians, who was a friend of mine, was from Brooklyn and had the classic Brooklyn features. For example, he walked fast, he talked fast, and he was always on the move. He approached me once in the hallway and asked, "Why don't you join us for the Rosary in the chapel?" I answered, "I usually pray the Rosary when I drive." He immediately fired back, "But, do you drive every day?" The answer was no. Sometimes, in the seminary, I only drove once or twice a week. I made a commitment many years ago, which was strengthened by Pope St. John Paul II's 2002 *Apostolic Letter on the Rosary of the Virgin Mary* to pray a daily Rosary. I try to pray the Rosary early in the day, as the days are sometimes very full and, thus, somewhat tiring. While I try daily to pray the Rosary before I fall asleep, I have been encouraged by that old adage that, if you fall asleep while praying the Rosary, the angels will finish it for you!

During my first year in the seminary, which was called pre-theology, we were not assigned to serve in a parish for the summer. We had the option of finding either a ministry or an educational opportunity. Somehow, I received a brochure of "A Christian Ministry in the National Parks." It sounded great. The summer chaplains served in national parks across the country. They usually had some regular job in the park or in a neighboring business and led Christian services on Sundays for campers and the staff of the park. As we had a number of national parks in our diocese, I thought that this would be a great opportunity. I received permission from the vocation director and applied for the program.

I then went to an orientation session in Indiana for the chaplains of that region. The founder of the ministry was an Episcopal priest. He took a liking to me at the orientation, and I was assigned to a very nice park in the North Carolina mountains with a weekday job at a local country club on the golf course crew. It really was a great summer, and the founder offered me a job to work with him for a couple of years in his national office. He just couldn't seem to understand that I had no intention of taking a couple of years off from the seminary to work in his interdenominational ministry. He said, "I will send you to seminaries all over the country to recruit for this ministry, and I especially believe that you will attract a lot of women ministers." That cracked me up! He even offered to call my bishop to inform him that I needed to take a couple of years off. He was very determined, and his attitude was that he didn't want to take no for an answer.

In addition to having three ecumenical services in the amphitheater every Sunday, I also served the Vigil Mass at one of our Catholic missions on Saturday evening. Most of my Sunday "flock" in the park were not Catholics, and I realized that many Catholic campers would prefer to drive to find a Catholic Mass in a neighboring town than to attend an ecumenical service in the park. Usually, my homilies were based on general Christian topics or Gospel stories such as the Good Samaritan, the Good Shepherd, or the Prodigal Son. I didn't introduce myself as a Catholic seminarian, but, if someone asked me where or what I was studying, I didn't deny it.

After the morning service on one of my first Sundays, a man approached me with a smile and said, "I detected hints of Lutheranism in this service, so I think that you are going to be a Lutheran minister. At that moment, a woman also approached and said, "No, I think that he is Methodist." I smiled and said, "I am preparing to be a Catholic priest." I could tell from their faces that they were both shocked. The woman then replied, "Well, you hide it very well!" Actually, I wasn't hiding anything.

In some ways, a priest is always on duty. I remember years ago, when I was heading to my parent's home on a cool Sunday night after a very busy weekend in the parish and mission in the North Carolina mountains. I was on a secondary highway, and, to my right, I saw a man hitchhiking. He had a duffle bag and looked to be wearing a navy cap. I thought that perhaps he was a sailor on leave trying to get home or trying to get back to his base. I turned around and stopped beside him on the shoulder of the road and asked, "Where are you going?" He told me where he was headed, but it was not near where I was going. I told him that I would bring him to an interstate that would be a better location for him to pick up a ride to his destination. I had just come from the parish after a late Mass and meeting and was still wearing my clerical shirt. He asked, "Are you a priest?"

I responded, "Yes."

He continued, "A Roman Catholic priest?"

"Yes," I affirmed.

He said, "I have never had a priest give me a ride before."

I asked if he was in the service, and he mentioned that he had been in the Coast Guard but was no longer on active duty. He got into my car, and we started off. I have picked up travelers over the years, and sometimes they ask for money or a good meal. This young man did not ask for money or food. He simply asked, "Father, may I make my confession?"

I said, "Sure."

He made his confession and received Absolution on a state highway going 55 mph. I'm pretty sure that I was only priest on that highway that night. Any number of people could have offered him a ride, but only a priest can grant Absolution.

Sometimes, I think that I may be able to identify a priest even in street clothes, and I wonder if someone may suspect that I am a priest in a setting outside of ministry. A good friend of mine from the seminary called me sometime after he had discontinued his formation to the priesthood to request if I would officiate his marriage. He is Canadian, and, after he returned home, he volunteered for some type of school counseling program and went to Guatemala on a mission trip. While he was there, he met the love of his life, and they had recently become engaged.

I accepted his invitation to travel to Guatemala for the wedding. He suggested that I try to arrive a few days early so that we could spend some time together, and he would show me around the area. The best man was a former college seminarian from St. Meinrad, and the three of us had a spent a lot of time in the gym playing basketball in earlier years. The groom, Wil, was, by far, the better player of us and probably could have played guard for a small college. The three of us visited the University of San Carlos, which is the oldest college in Central America. As we walked through the campus, some students were choosing sides for a pickup basketball game on an outdoor court. We were just visiting the campus and had not intended to play ball and were not dressed for it.

The timing was incredible, and we got on a team for the first game. This was about twenty years ago, so I was in better shape, but the students were at least fifteen years younger than me and had high energy. We played hard and, after a while, Wil cycled out of a game. By this time, a small crowd had gathered, and they were watching their fellow students playing with these three North Americans.

Wil spoke with a couple of the students on the sidelines. He pointed to me and asked, "What kind of job do you think that guy has?"

A student responded, "He is a security guard."

Wil said with a smile, "No, he is a priest."

The student didn't believe it and said, "Well, he looks like a security guard, but he's certainly not a PRIEST!" (¡No es un sacerdote!)

Interestingly, there was another time when someone also thought that I was a security guard. I was invited by former NASCAR racer and parishioner Bobby Allison to accompany him to the Charlotte Motor Speedway to watch the race in his suite in the Speedway Club tower. Before the race started, Bobby, his brother Donnie, and several other former racers and racing officials were gathered in a room for autographs, conversation, and a few tall tales. While Bobby and Donnie signed their books and sold memorabilia, I stood quietly on one side of the room overlooking the scene. I was dressed casually and was wearing a dark ball cap. Someone noticed me and came over and asked, "Are you part of the security detail?"

I just smiled and replied, "No, I am with the Allison's."

The "security guard" with retired racers,
Donnie and Bobby Allison at the
Speedway Club in 2018

CHAPTER 47

Jesus, the Prince of Peace

For a child is born to us, a son is given us; upon his shoulder dominion rests. They name him Won-der-Counselor, God-Hero, Father-Forever, Prince of Peace. His dominion is vast and forever peaceful.
—ISAIAH 9:5–6: FIRST READING AT
THE MASS AT NIGHT ON CHRISTMAS EVE

As our Lord is the Prince of Peace, news of violence, especially against the innocent, certainly shakes me. Over recent years, it seems as though senseless acts of violence, especially shootings, have become more common in our midst. After learning of these incidents, I think of the extended pain of the families, friends, emergency responders, and members of the community. The reports also remind me of how I had to respond to a tragedy in my pastoral territory when I was still pretty new in the priesthood.

I was at our diocesan priests' retreat in Maggie Valley, when I received word of five men who had been killed in the small rural community of Mangum, North Carolina. The local officials were looking for a priest who spoke Spanish. I left the retreat for the 230-mile drive back to my mission in Biscoe. It was a journey from the peacefulness and beauty of the North Carolina mountains to a situation of sadness and grief. Upon my return, I learned more information about the killings. Eight men had lived together in a farmhouse and worked as agricultural workers. On the previous Sunday afternoon, two of the housemates, who were brothers, opened fire on the others with a high-powered rifle and a pistol. Five were killed, and one was wounded. The apparent motive was robbery. I officiated the funeral service with all five caskets present in the small community center of Mangum.

Many of the Hispanic farmworkers from the region attended the service arriving by bus. I don't think that many actually knew those who had been slain, but they came because they could identify with them and wanted to pray for them. Some of those who had been killed were fathers and were working in the fields of North Carolina to provide for their families back home in Mexico.

The man who survived the attack began to attend the Mass at our mission in Biscoe, but he never seemed to recover from the tragedy of being shot by coworkers and seeing his brother and friends murdered. During my time at the mission, he always looked troubled and pale. He became a witness for law enforcement officials and was instrumental in the identification and arrest of the two brothers in Mexico. It is our prayer that people will turn to the Prince of Peace in our troubled world.

The Fifth Commandment states: "You shall not kill" (Ex 20:13), and the *Catechism* (no. 2258) teaches:

Human life is sacred because from its beginning it involves the creative action of God and it remains forever in a special relationship with the Creator, who is its sole end. God alone is the Lord of life from its beginning until its end: no one can under any circumstance claim for himself the right directly to destroy an innocent human being.

The teaching of the Church is that the innocent should always be protected. This includes those in the womb, the elderly, the sick, and children in schools. The Church acknowledges legitimate defense for oneself and for others, and she appreciates dedicated and ethical law enforcement officials and military personnel and encourages that they use only the force that is necessary to accomplish their mission. Of course, we recognize their great challenge to make decisions in a fraction of a second.

Our prayers are with the victims of violence, with those who grieve the loss of loved ones and with those who strive to protect and serve.

CHAPTER 48

Leslie

For whoever does the will of my heavenly Father is
my brother, and sister, and mother.
—MATTHEW 12:50

For this chapter, I yield to my mother who paid tribute to my sister Leslie in this reflection from almost thirty years ago. Leslie was called from this life in 1991 at the age of twenty. My mother died seven years later in 1998. May they rest in peace.

Dear Leslie,

You slipped so effortlessly and painlessly into my life in May 1970. I remember so vividly looking into your face as the nurse held you up. I was seeing a face that I had seen before—mine (in baby pictures). I could hardly believe the words, "It's a girl!" After four boys! My own girl! Later, when we were reunited in my room after a tedious stay in the recovery room, I was thrilled and apprehensive to have you to myself. I began the long list of calling friends to tell them I finally had a girl! But why hadn't the doctor come in, and why were the nurses so quiet when I asked? And then your father came in to tell me that the doctor said that you were "Mongoloid" - (the term they used back then). That word filled my evening. I realized that my initial plans had changed. My new daughter needed me in a special way. A new friend taught me a lot over the next few months. She told me that my daughter would learn to do many things. She would run and jump and be a contributor to society.

When you were only six months old, our house caught on fire. While we all escaped, I realized that we could have lost you from the smoke. I felt that you were not meant to die at that time. I was so right. You were meant to do many things. You progressed quickly and were soon walking alone. One skill followed another.

One day, I picked you up from the special needs preschool, and you were hamming it up with a boy confined to a wheelchair. He was laughing at your antics. I realized that you had reached out of yourself to someone else. I always tried to educate the public about your condition, Down Syndrome. You were always an overachiever. We were pals. We went everywhere together and were seen around town as a pair. As you got older, we shared clothes. As the years went by, you were always there when I needed a hug. You instinctively knew when your brothers needed a kind word or a hug. Everyone loved you. When you got sick, I couldn't believe that you wouldn't respond to the medicine. When we found you lifeless, it was unbelievable. You had slipped so quietly into our lives. How could you slip so quietly out of our lives? Leslie! I miss you so!

When we arranged your funeral, we didn't know what kind of crowd would be present at the memorial service for a twenty-year old retarded child who died after a five-day illness. More than 250 people crowded the funeral home. Some only knew you through the YMCA, the American Legion parties, the Special Olympics, the school system, and the soup kitchen where you worked. You demonstrated that you had been born with a mission, and you did your job very well.

Very well indeed. I am so proud of you, my darling Leslie. I love you.

Jo Lawlor

CHAPTER 49

World Day of Prayer for Vocations

He said to them, "The harvest is abundant but the
laborers are few; so ask the master of the harvest to
send out laborers for his harvest.
—LUKE 10:2

The Fourth Sunday of Easter is known as Good Shepherd Sunday. Each year on this Sunday, the Gospel passage is taken from the tenth chapter of the Gospel of John, which includes our Lord's teaching on the Good Shepherd. For example, in Year C, the Gospel includes: "Jesus said, 'My sheep hear my voice; I know them, and they follow me. I give them eternal life, and they shall never perish.'" On this Sunday, throughout the Church, we are all encouraged to pray for and to support vocations to the priesthood. Pope Francis, as did his predecessors, continues to encourage the faithful to pray for the sanctity of the clergy and for a spiritual renewal.

All those who have been entrusted with pastoral ministry have our Lord as the model shepherd. We should always remember that the flock is the Lord's. As a pastor, I recognize the many ways that I fall short of the model of the Good Shepherd. As we celebrate the World Day of Prayer for Vocations, we pray for a positive response to the call from God to serve in a religious vocation. As one who has been called, I can attest, "It is a wonderful life!" Just before my ordination, Bishop Curlin wrote to me the following:

Mark, as you enter your first priestly assignment, I
encourage you to maintain a close identity with Christ

> *by using every means possible in strengthening your*
> *oneness with Him. From my own personal experience, I*
> *can assure you that it is essential that a priest center his*
> *life around the Eucharist and in daily prayer. . . . I beg*
> *you to make charity the foundation of everything you do*
> *in priestly ministry. Our world is experiencing so much*
> *pain that it cries out for the compassion and kindness of*
> *Christ, whose representative you are.*

While I served on the diocesan vocations board, I interviewed several applicants for our seminarian program. As a pastor, I supervised some of our seminarians who are now my brother priests. I am convinced that the Lord continues to call men to this vocation. I am sincerely thankful for all of the ministries in the Church. We work together. The Church, however, needs priests for such sacred sacraments as the Eucharist, Penance, Confirmation (RCIA), and the Anointing of the Sick. Let us pray that, after hearing the call, more will respond yes to a vocation to the priesthood.

On Good Shepherd Sunday, I especially reflect on the gift of the priesthood with great humility. Jesus taught, "The harvest is abundant, but the laborers are few; so ask the master of the harvest to send out laborers for his harvest" (Mt 9:37–38). We are all called to pray for and to support religious vocations.

I recently read the story of Mrs. Eliza Vaughan who took this message to heart. She was an Englishwoman from a strong Protestant family who was received into the Catholic Church after her marriage to Colonel John Vaughan. Her conversion to Catholicism went against the desires of her family. Eliza was convinced of the power of prayer, and she spent one hour every day in the presence of the Blessed Sacrament praying for vocations from her own family. John and Eliza's oldest son, Herbert, felt the call to ordained ministry at the age of sixteen. After he shared this with his parents, Eliza's response was, "Child, I have known it for a long time." John, however, was initially not so excited. He had hoped that Herbert would go on to a prestigious military career. He eventually gave his assent to his son's calling. At the time, John certainly did not know that his oldest son would one day be the Archbishop of Westminster and the founder of a missionary order. He also did not know that Herbert would become a cardinal of the Church, and he certainly could not have foreseen that his oldest son would one day ordain their youngest son, John, to the priesthood. John, Jr. would also become a bishop. John and Eliza Vaughan had fourteen children. Of the thirteen children that survived infancy, six became priests, and four became nuns in religious orders. The Vaughan family of nineteenth-century England was certainly spiritually sound, and they left a positive impact on the Church. [5]

Prayer is important. Are there many people today who pray with the same dedication as Eliza?

[5] See "Triumph of the Heart: Mothers for Priests." Family of Mary, 2005 (I), No. 31, 12–14; www.familiemariens.info/html/en/pdf/31.pdf.

CHAPTER 50

Transitions and Mentors

No disciple is superior to the teacher; but when fully
trained, every disciple will be like his teacher.
—LUKE 6:40

At the time a priest receives an assignment, he usually does not have a clear idea of how long the assignment will last. I have seen pastors who have served for twenty years in the same parish and others would were transferred after only one year or so. Spending a lot of time in a parish affords one such pastoral experiences as officiating a marriage, baptizing the children of that couple, and then giving the children their First Holy Communion.

As a pastor, I have had the responsibility of mentoring and supervising sixteen parochial vicars and nineteen seminarians. I hope that I have been able to help them along their journey. The term mentor is defined as a wise and trusted counselor or advisor. I am very thankful for the good mentors that I had during my time as a seminarian and parochial vicar. As a seminarian, I looked up to my former pastor at Sacred Heart Parish in Salisbury, Fr. Tom Clements. He served in Salisbury for many years, and he welcomed me to the pastoral team whenever I was home from the seminary. I had been an altar server during Fr. Tom's first assignment in Salisbury in the early seventies.

I spent one summer with Msgr. Anthony Kovacic at Queen of the Apostles in Belmont. Fr. Anthony, a native of Slovenia, worked very hard, and he shared with me many stories of his studies in Rome and his early days in North Carolina. He had a great memory for details, and he also demonstrated a great dedication to the Church.

Msgr. Thomas Burke of County Mayo, Ireland, was my supervisor the summer before my ordination. He was truly a holy priest who spent many hours in prayer. He had been a missionary in Africa, and he spoke with joy of his experiences of preaching to "first generation Christians."

After my ordination, I spent one year as parochial vicar at Holy Family Church in Clemmons and then one year at St. Leo's in Winston Salem before I was sent out on my own to the mission in Biscoe. I learned some valuable lessons about being a pastor by observing my mentors.

A few years ago, I was saddened to learn of the death of my good friend and brother priest, Fr. Richard T. McCue. Earlier that year, he had celebrated the fifty-fifth anniversary of his priestly ordination. I first met the good padre when I was a seminarian. He welcomed me to his pastoral territory in Spruce Pine and Linville in the summer of 1991. He represented the image of the "kindhearted and hospitable pastor." Any seminarian who showed up at his parish was treated to a steak dinner and received a complimentary tank of gas! Fr. McCue vested me at my diaconate ordination in 1994. He supported our capital campaign while I was a pastor in Charlotte with a couple of generous checks. Before his death, I had written to him to say that I was looking forward to seeing him at our diocesan priest's retreat. He had moved to the Northeast but usually returned to North Carolina for our priest's retreat.

I do miss him.

With my mentors,
Msgr. Burke and Msgr. Kovacic
Requiescat in Pace

With Fr. Richard T. McCue, a marine, navy
chaplain, faithful priest and pastor, and a good friend.
Requiescat in Pace

CHAPTER 51

We Are Family

For this reason I kneel before the Father,
from whom every family in heaven and on earth is
named,
—EPHESIANS 3:14-15

I read an article in the *Old Farmer's Almanac* some time ago that stated that no two people on earth are further apart than fiftieth cousins and that most people are much closer than that.

In the Book of Genesis, Eve is called the "mother of all the living" (Gn 3:20). Interestingly, Dr. Spencer Wells, an expert on DNA, writes of an "Eve" as the biological mother of all living persons in his book *The Journey of Man: A Genetic Odyssey.* In other words, all living people are her descendants and, therefore, we are all related. Science recognizes and agrees with the principals expressed in the Scriptures that we have a common ancestor.

Every person may affirm that "we are family." Dr. Wells, a geneticist and anthropologist, shows through the study of DNA samples from people throughout the world of the migrations of humans over the past 50,000+ years and of our common human parentage. I found his work to be very interesting, and I have watched his programs on this topic on PBS and on YouTube over the years. In fact, I was inspired to have my DNA analyzed after learning of this technology. It is something that my father and I talked about.

Many families have stories of ancestors. In our family, for example, one grandmother said that the Lawlor's were descendants of an Irish king. On the others side, there was a story of English nobility and that one ancestor, John Hart, had signed the Declaration of Independence. My grandmother related how some of her people were Prussians and that the only way to suppress the Prussians was to kill them! She also told me (in a very low voice) that some of our relatives had died at St. Elizabeth Psychiatric Hospital in Washington, D.C.

Originally, I was looking at my heritage from a purely mathematical equation. As I had two great-grandparents who were natives of Ireland and two great-grandparents who were natives of Italy, I always said that I was one-fourth Irish and one-fourth Italian. It seemed like easy fractions.

I finally sent my saliva sample to ancestry.com, and I anxiously awaited the analysis and results. When I received them, I was somewhat surprised by the breakdown of my DNA. According to the analysis, I am 34% Irish, 27% Scottish, 16% of England and Northwestern Europe (including The Netherlands, Belgium, and Luxembourg), 15% of Germanic Europe, 6% of Northern Italy, and 2% of Eastern Europe (including Russia, Hungary, Slovenia, and Ukraine). I have since learned that even children of the same parents may not have an identical DNA breakdown.

My DNA make-up is a little more complicated than I imagined! In my family tree, I have found veterans of the army and navy, a printer, a shoemaker, a fireman, a statesman, an electrician, a cabinet maker, a tailor, a dressmaker, some musicians, an opera singer, artists, and even a seminarian, who apparently ran away from the seminary. One grandmother told me that we had family members on both sides of the Civil War. Someone once told me that we could probably find a horse thief in the family as well!

We are linked together genetically and in Faith. In Baptism, we enter that Family of God. Jesus is our Lord and Brother. The great commandments are to love God and to love neighbor. It may be helpful to us to recognize that our neighbor is also a member of our family.

The Church is the Family of God and the Mystical Body of Christ.

CHAPTER 52

Twenty-five Years . . . Already?

Your statutes become my songs wherever I make my home.
—PSALM 119:54

L
ast year, I noted that twenty-five years had passed since my ordination to the priesthood and that it had been thirty-two years since my midnight drive from my parent's home in North Carolina to Hartford, Kentucky, to begin my religious formation. The time has passed so quickly that sometimes I have to think twice about the number of years. My ordination to the priesthood was about ten years after I first heard the call of the Lord. I discerned the calling for three years while working as an engineer, and then spent about seven years in religious formation, which began with the Glenmary Home Missioners.

Since my ordination, I have celebrated the funerals for both of my parents, an aunt, and both grandmothers. My sister, Leslie, and one niece, Michaela, died while I was in formation, and I helped with both of their funerals.

At my Mass of Ordination on June 3, 1995, Bishop Curlin reminded the three us (Fr. Jim Collins, Fr. Eric Houseknecht, and myself) that the step that we were taking was "a mystery to the world." He told us that we would be entrusted with an "awesome responsibility," but that we would have a wonderful life in Christ. He instructed us to be men of prayer, the Eucharist, Penance, and charity. He encouraged us to be a "visible sign of God's eternal mercy." He let us know that we would share in the joys of the faithful and also in their anguish and grief. Bishop Curlin preached that the Gospel message is that of Jesus, and that we are called to be His messengers. At the moment of ordination, I felt the power of God change my life. I will always humbly thank God for the gift of the priesthood. I know that I have been tremendously blessed.

I once heard one of my former pastors, Msgr. Anthony Kovacic say, "I have always received more than I needed and certainly more than I ever deserved." I can echo that sentiment every day. It is still hard for me to fathom that God called such an unlikely candidate as me to this glorious vocation. The words of Jesus ring true for me: "It was not you who chose me, but I who chose you and appointed you to go and bear fruit that will remain, so that whatever you ask the Father in my name, He may give you" (Jn 15:16).

I am thankful for those who encouraged me in my parish assignments, for the school children who wrote to me while I was studying at St. Meinrad Seminary, and for the family members and parishioners who assured me of their prayers during my formation and studies. I am sincerely thankful for all the support that I have received over the years. There are people who still encourage, nurture, and support vocations. Just a few days ago, someone said to me, "Father, thank you for being a priest." I find such statements to be very uplifting! All those who have been entrusted with pastoral ministry have our Lord as the model shepherd. We should always remember that the flock is the Lord's. Perhaps many of us pastors recognize the ways that we fall short of the model of the Good Shepherd. As one who has been called, I can attest, "It is a wonderful life!"

Over the past twenty-six years, I have strived to faithfully live this calling. I have been to places, met people, and had experiences that I would never have dreamed of. I have blessed families, cars, bicycles, buses, boats, dogs, cats, horses, homes, restaurants, classrooms, and even a tortilleria (where they make tortillas). I have celebrated Masses in parishes, schools, basilicas, shrines, cathedrals, homes, hotels, fields, prisons, boats, at the House of Mary in Ephesus, at the Chapel of Tepeyac in Mexico where our Lady of Guadalupe gave the roses to St. Juan

Diego, the Grotto in Lourdes, the Site of the apparitions in Fatima, the altar of Pope St. John Paul II, at the great Basilica of St. Anne de Beaupré in Canada and at the tomb of our Lord in Jerusalem. I celebrated the Mass in the ruins in the ancient section of Corinth where the apostle Paul had once preached. I have visited mansions, apartments, trailers, jails, middle class homes, coal and copper mines, farms and ranches, monasteries, convents, vineyards, tobacco fields, the Apostolic Palace and even the Nunciature in Washington, D.C., twice! I have prayed in the cave on the island of Patmos where the beloved disciple, St. John, received the vision for the Book of Revelation. I have prayed invocations at dinners, banquets, ecumenical services, meetings of the City Council and the County Commissioners, and even at an NFL game. I participated in an exorcism in Mexico, which was quite shocking to me. I have baptized thousands and officiated hundreds of weddings and funerals and given blessings to couples on anniversaries of all lengths: 25, 40, 50, 60, and even 70 years! I have prayed the Rosary with parishioners in many parishes, with religious sisters, with children, and with a saint (JPII). I have been a cruise ship chaplain in the Atlantic and the Pacific Oceans. As a priest, I have been to mountains, beaches and jungles, to the top of church towers and cupolas, and down to the subterranean catacombs and crypts. I once prayed the Liturgy of the Hours on the top of a Mayan pyramid in Mexico that had been a place of human sacrifices to the sun. I have been to a great number of hospitals, nursing homes, hospice units, cemeteries, and even to a few morgues for sacraments and blessings. I have been to the tombs of many saints, including the St Junípero Serra, the Apostles Sts. Peter and Paul in Rome and that of my own patron, St. Mark, in Venice. These years have been quite fulfilling.

Every day in the parish is a new day of joy and grace. Many thanks for your prayers and support.

St. John Vianney, Patron Saint of Priests, Please Pray for Us.

You are welcome to view some of Fr. Mark's videos on YouTube including the very popular, "A Day in the Life of a Parish Priest." Search under that title or Fr Mark Lawlor.

Entering St. Gabriel's
for my priestly ordination
with my parents on June 3,
1995.
As a priest, I celebrated
both of their funerals.